GO TO HELL.
PLEASE?

A CALL FOR REVIVAL!

"Plus 53 bonus articles "From the Heart"

TIMOTHY J. HALL

Pastor;
Gully Springs Baptist Church
(Church)
PO Box 745
2824 Hwy 90 West
(Home)
PO Box 1371
Bonifay, Florida 32428
(850) 547-3920 Church
(850) 547-5228 Home

E-mail; timhall_2000@yahoo.com

CHURCH, GO TO HELL! PLEASE?
A CALL FOR REVIVAL!
by Timothy J. Hall

First Edition

Printed in the United States of America

ISBN 978-1-60791-219-4

Request for information should be addressed to
Timothy J. Hall
PO Box 1371
Bonifay, Florida 32425
850-547-5228
timhall_2000@yahoo.com

All Scripture quotations, unless otherwise indicated, are from The Holy Bible, KJV, King James Version, Third Edition, Electronic Edition STEP Files, Copyright © 1998, Parsons Technology Inc. Cedar Rapids Iowa.

1. Religion: Spirituality General
2. Self-Help: Spiritual
3. Religion: Christian Life - Personal Growth
4. Religion: Inspirational

www.xulonpress.com

TABLE OF CONTENTS

Title Page   Page #

This book is dedicated to;

First,
to my Savior and Lord, who purchased my Salvation
on an old Rugged Cross.

Secondly,
to my wife Judy and my parents Leon & Shirley Hall, who
have always encouraged me to follow the Lord in whatever
direction He was leading. And to Joy Younavjak who
worked with me for over eight years as a secretary, and
editor of my weekly writings, and who is a dear friend.

Thirdly,
to the churches, that the Lord has used to help mold me into
a usable vessel for my Lord.

Most of all, this book is dedicated to you who read this
book, may the Lord give you the burden that He has given
me to reach out to lost and dying that they might also know
the joy of Eternal Life.

Chapter 1

THE
PROBLEM

As we look around us, we can all easily say, "We are living in the most exciting days since Jesus Himself walked upon the face of the earth." No, it's not exciting because of the marvel of electricity or the combustible engine and the power that these things have afforded us. Yes, these great inventions have brought even greater and more wonderful inventions into our lives. Because of these things, men are finding ways everyday to bring greater luxury and more entertainment and ease into our lives.

Today, virtually everyone can travel extensively and enjoy this beautiful world God has created. With the technology of today, we can enjoy it all with very little effort on our part, whereas seventy-five years ago it would have taken a great effort. Rapid transit has truly changed the way we think about travel.

Telephones and computers have opened up means of communication and ways of gathering information that still boggles the mind. No, these things are not what make this day such an exciting day. What makes this day so exciting is that we live in a day, in which Christ is eagerly waiting for the Father to say,

"Son, Go get Your Bride."
In the New Testament alone, the second coming of Christ is mentioned 318 times. We as born-again believers, Disciples of Christ, should be excited and working like crazy to lead the world to Christ. For He is coming, whether we are ready or not, at His appointed time.

The early church grew tremendously just because a few had witnessed His ascension and heard His promise to return. As they gazed into the heavens looking for just one more glimpse of Him, two angels appeared and said, *"Why do you stand here gazing into the sky? You've got work to do, there's a world to win."* (**Acts 1:9-11** Paraphrased) They then followed the instructions of Christ, and waited on the Holy Spirit. When they were empowered by the Holy Spirit, they then went into the world preaching, teaching and baptizing just as He had commanded.

That same excitement that turned the world upside down, will still build great churches today. For it is not excitement about new technology, theology, theories or new discoveries, but an excitement about the truth, the truth that Heaven and Hell are real, that Christ has purchased The Church with a great price and is soon coming after His Bride.

It seems the zeal and drive to win the world for Christ has been lost in most local churches, because we have forgotten what the precious blood of Christ purchased us from. **Luke 16:19-31** gives us a very clear picture of Hell. Luke not only describes the torments and the loneliness of Hell that we don't want to admit exists, but Luke also shares with us information about the people and the activities that they are involved in there.

If you will take a close look at the activities that Luke describes are taking place in Hell, you will be surprised to find that these are the same activities that the Lord promised He would bless, if His people were involved in them. The shame of it all is, in Hell these activities are useless.

**Putting it simply,
there are activities taking place in Hell
that need to be taking place in
our churches today,
and a lot of things going on in our
local churches
that belong in Hell.**

The Question?

Have you ever wondered how churches go for a year or even years without baptizing a single person of any age? Yet we know that there are thousands of churches across America and around the world that continually report that in the past year they have had no one to walk down the aisle of the church and ask Christ to become their Lord and Savior.

I know, and I hope you know, that a person does not have to walk down an aisle of a church to receive eternal life. That any place where a person may ask Christ to be the Lord of their life, becomes an altar. Yet many churches continue to report no baptisms. Again I am assuming that these churches claiming to be New Testament Christian churches are teaching the Bible, which teaches that once a person becomes a believer, they will follow the Lord in believer's baptism as He commanded, to testify to the world outwardly, what has taken place inwardly.

Since there are no reported baptisms in these churches, this seems to say, that for some reason, the church members (the disciples) are not leading anyone to Christ in their homes, in their places of work, while on hunting trips or fishing trips, or even while shopping or sitting with friends. It seems as though everyone is leaving Christ and Christianity at the church house. They seem to expect those who are lost to come to Christ, without anyone taking the opportunity to introduce those they love to Him.

**It seems as if those who call themselves Christians,
do not want to share Heaven with anyone else.**

Excuses

There's an unasked question that the older local church keeps trying to answer. Their answers are simply excuses for the local church. The question is, why are large, small, rural and city churches closing their doors across America? Why, are people not attending Sunday school, Bible studies and Worship services at the local church?

The real question they should be asking is, why is it that less than 5% of the average (active) church membership ever attempt to witness for Christ? Why do the other 95% never even attempt to share the Good News of the Gospel?

The answer to the last question is wrapped up in that one word, "Excuses", which belong in Hell, with the activities that are now very active in most of our churches. The list of activities that have found their way into our churches that don't belong there begin with: gossip, power struggles, and traditions. These activities that have entered into our churches belong in Hell.

Everywhere I go, I hear the same statement. From small community churches, medium size churches and churches sitting in the midst of large cities, I hear the same excuse over and over again, *"No one is interested in going to church anymore."* The churches *that* were once large and full, are now empty and even closed or closing. Yet there are billions of people who have not yet received Christ as their

Lord. The world's population continues to grow at an alarming faster rate than the church. As you look at the figures, and listen to what is being said, it should make any born-again Christian begin to ask the question, "**WHY, are <u>they</u> not interested?**"

Before we take a very special trip through Hell, where we will see the things that are taking place there, that need to be taking place in our churches, let's take a moment in this first chapter to look at some of these excuses that have found their way in the church that need to be in Hell.

<u>Excuse # 1 - Not Enough People</u>

When you begin to ask individuals why their church is not growing, I have literally been surprised, and I know many pastors have also been, when that question was answered with this statement, "*there are just not enough people to fill all the churches*". Are they saying there are too many churches?

With some quick and easy research, either by going to the county court house, chamber of commerce, or city hall, there you can find out how many people live in a given area and how many churches are in that area. In most areas where this type of research has been done, it has shown that there are at least 600 people per church. That's including all the "so-called" churches in the area. When you begin to subtract those that are cults and are not Biblically sound, you find out that there are from 1,500 to 2,000 people per church building in almost any community. The research that I have done comes from rural communities, not cities. In cities there are more people per square mile and fewer churches, thus the number per church would even be greater. Also in these areas, where I have found that there are 1,500 people per church building, I also found out that the average church in these areas usually only seat 150 to 200 people.

**So again I ask the question,
"Why are the churches not filled?"**

In my simple mind as I read, **Matthew 25:14-30**, the story where the traveling master leaves his talents to his servants, it seems that God is speaking to us today. Saying, that if He has led a group of His children to build a church in a community, He has also has given them the responsibility to reach that community for Him. So as simple minds would think, God has given each of these churches the responsibility and will hold them accountable to Him for not reaching them. We must see it as our commissioned responsibility from God to strive to reach all people for Him, then train them and support them as they grow in Him. Remember the Great Commission says for us to Go to them;

**And He said to them,
"Go into all the world
and preach the gospel to every creature."
Mark 16:15.**

When I examine the statement,
"There are not enough people",
after much research and prayer, I come to the conclusion that what they are actually saying is,
"There are not enough, of the right kind, of people."
(Speaking of their kind of people, people like them).
To that statement I would have to reply,
**Nowhere in the Bible does it teach that God would build His church out of the right kind of people,
but it does teach that He would build it of
All People.**

Excuse # 2 - Not Interested

We have now proven that there are enough people to fill all churches to capacity. We have also taken notice that all churches should be increasing in attendance and baptizing believers into the family of God. Because population continues to increase, and if we are faithful to follow our Lord's Great Commission, He will be faithful to give increase.

We now should turn to the statement, *"No one is interested in going to church anymore."* This statement should be turned into a question. *Why are people not interested in coming to our church?* Here's another question for you to consider, *has there ever been a time in history when people who did not know Christ personally, had an interest in coming to the local church house?* If you truly ask yourself this question and research history, you will find the answer is no. There has never been a time in history when men and women who did not know Christ personally had an interest in the church. Nor has Christ ever instructed the lost to come to the church, but He commissioned (ordered) the church to go to them. So, we then must come to the conclusion,

**The problem is not that lost people
do not have an interest in the church,
but that those who claim to be the church
are lazy, disobedient
and are not interested
in going out as the Lord has commanded.**

Excuse # 3 - Competition

Then others come to the conclusion that there is just too much competition for an individual's time in the day and age in which we live. Are they saying that they think that there is more competition for a person's time today than there were in the past? May I first qualify the statement? Are they saying that the church in Acts, where the Lord added to the church daily, as many as 3,000 souls in one day, that they had no competition? If so, boy, are they wrong!

Yes, the early church had some awesome competition, competition as we are yet to experience here in America. We whine and bellyache about our government and the way that Christians are ignored and ridiculed. Do you realize that the "saints-of-old" feared for their lives? And they had a very good reason to fear for their lives. The kings and rulers of their time were willing to, and even had, Christians killed because of their testimony or for preaching the gospel. That would definitely keep people from wanting to come to church, wouldn't you agree? The church as we know it was not established and had not earned the respectful place that it now holds in our communities of today. They did not have the entire Word of God readily available to each of them. Even the so-called religious leaders of that time were out to destroy the Christian church. Remember they were the ones who crucified Christ. False Prophets arose preaching another gospel, but saying they were of Christ, thus confusing the people.

Their time was also very valuable to them then, as ours is today, or even more so then than now. They had large families to support along with jobs and careers. Be sure not to forget they had their sports, entertainment and hobbies also. In reality the church of the twenty-first century in comparison to the first century church of Acts, has nothing to complain about.

The real question or comparison that should be made is:
<u>Where are our priorities?</u>

Oh yes, I know you've heard about the "good ole days" here in America. The days when Sunday came, everyone would jump in the community buggy on the way to church and stay all day. You say those days were so much simpler. But, just stop and think a minute. The "good ole days" are never as good as we remember, because we were children.

As we remember our childhood, things are always bigger, larger and better than they actually were. If you could call back from the grave, those who actually lived in those so called *"Good Ole Days"*, the stories you would hear would probably amaze you. You would hear that those days were very long days with short nights, and that not everyone went to church.

As you spoke to those who did attend church, you would find that they were concerned about worship and family. They would say they had to put their priorities in order. They would say they made time for the important things in life. If they could come and speak to us today, they would probably scorn the best of us for the life of ease we now live, with so many wonderful opportunities to serve the Lord, but yet we are so lazy about His work.

The first thing we need to see as a church is, the Bible does not say that the lost should come to church.

But, *Christ sent the Apostles out*, to preach and to teach. He said for Christians to go into the world, to be a peculiar and separated people, but not an indifferent people. Remember He referred to The Church as the salt and the light of the world.

Think about what that means. Meat is not normally applied to the salt to cure the meat, but the salt is applied to the meat, that the meat might become cured and seasoned.

Darkness does not invade light, but light invades that which is dark.

So it is not the responsibility of the darkness to come to the place of light, but for those who dwell in the light and reflect the greater light, to take the light to those who dwell in darkness.

Fishers of Men

May we ask another question? Why are so few coming to know Christ and why are there no real revivals? Instead of going to people and getting their excuses, let's go to the scripture for guidance.

In **Matthew 4:19**, Jesus came to Peter and Andrew as they were fishing for fish and said to them,

"Follow Me, and I will make you fishers of men."

***First* we notice that He spoke to them in terms that they could understand**. You see, they were fishermen and understood fishing.

***Secondly,* the part that they did not understand, "fishing for men," He then led them to follow Him so He could begin to train them.**

Real fishermen know that fishing is not as simple as most think it is, (those who don't fish). Fishing is an enjoyable sport, but like any other sport, to really enjoy it, is to be good at it. To be good at it means one must continue to work at it. Fishing takes courage, patience, training and the right equipment. Then and only then can one truly enjoy the sport of fishing. Until one has the courage to get on the water where the fish are and the courage to get the training that is needed to be successful, he or she will not enjoy the sport of fishing. Most training is obtained through experience and learning from others who have more experience than you. A good fisherman not only has to have the courage to go to the water where the fish are, he also has to have the courage to both learn by experience and through others. He also has to have the courage to invest more than just his time in this sport, but also courage to invest his money to get the best equipment for the job, equipment that will get the job done right and most rewarding. Then he has to have the courage to have patience. Patience to wait, as well as to have faith in the bait that he is casting, will reach the desired target.

When Jesus said to Peter and Andrew, *"Follow me and I will make you fishers of men,"* they knew it was going to be enjoyable, but they also knew they had a lot to learn. Actually they spent three years getting the training they needed from the Master. Training that not only involved watching, but training that also involved hands on experience and mistakes. They learned of the value of the equipment of which they had been entrusted. Then they received the training that they needed to get the most of not only their investment, but the great investment in which Christ had put in it Himself and would put in them.

It seems that if those who the master hand picked, needed three years of training and hands-on experience under His leadership, then we too need to learn how to get the most out of our tools. Would it not help us today, to realize, not only the importance of following Him but also the joy of being all that He would have us to be? That joy comes from being trained and getting experience under the direction of others who have been faithful to the Word of

God, alone with hours of studying the manual (the Bible), and hours of communicating with the Master in prayer.

We must first begin to follow.

Chapter 2

A
SPECIAL
TRIP

On Public TV there is a children's program that I enjoyed watching with my children, [2]"The Magic School Bus." On this program the children at the school get into their School Bus, as the bus changes sizes and shapes, the children enjoy travel through books, countries, flowers and even the internal parts of the human body such as: the digestive system, the lungs and the heart. Anything that might help children have a greater understanding of their studies.

What do you think would take place in the local church if each of us could take such a trip through Hell? If we could have a first hand experience and actually see friends, fellow workers, and relatives who have already died, and who will die and go to Hell, if we don't take the Gospel to them. If we could for just a moment feel the pain, and depression that they are experiencing, because their eternal destination is sealed, for they will spend eternity dying, but yet never dying.

After taking such a trip, it seems we would come back with a greater desire to be equipped and a greater courage to go fishing (for people). If we the Church could take such a trip, it would seem that the pastor would never have to beg Christians to come to Sunday School to study God's Word, to worship services to praise our Savior, to training seminars to be trained that we might be more effective for Him, nor would anyone ever have to be asked to come to prayer meetings to communicate with our Best Friend, because there would be a great desire, a great HUNGER to be equipped, to share "The Good News" of Christ our Lord with others.

If each Christian would take this trip, there would be no need for the lost to take such a trip, EVER! Because sleeping Christians would be woke up, and cold churches would be set on fire for God. The song service and the sermons would change; our services would begin to include enthusiasm, praise, real prayer, real worship to God and encouragement for each other. All because a visit to Hell, would make the price that was paid on Calvary so much more precious to each of us, we would then realize that Hell is not the place that murders, homosexuals, abortionist, liars and thieves go to. But that Hell is where sinners who have rejected Christ will spend eternity without any hope.

When will we begin to realize that Hell is a real place? When we begin to realize the reason we are not going to Hell, is because our name has been written in the Lamb's Book of Life.

**It's not because of who we are,
that we are not going to Hell.
But because of our acceptance
of the work of Christ on Calvary.**

When we really begin to realize this, then we will naturally begin to rejoice, and begin to get a great hunger to share this wonderful gift we have with those who we love. Could you imagine our churches packed with disciples, disciples who are training because they have a great hunger to be able to share this wonderful gift of Salvation with someone else?

It seems we have become so wrapped up in church work we have lost the true reason for the church. As [2]"The parable of the Fisherman" told by Robert L. Hamblin, Robert *told about a group of fishermen who became very interested in the art of fishing. They developed equipment and methods for fishing. They formed fishing societies and went everywhere promoting fishing. They became so busy with the art of fishing that they had no time to fish.* It's so true, sometimes we get so busy doing busy things that we don't have time to do the mission the Lord has left us to do.

**If we could take a Magic Church Bus trip
through Hell,
we would soon learn,**
*The reason our churches are not filled,
is not because of the condition of the world,
but the condition of the church.*

When we begin to read the Word of God, His letters to His children, we find that such a trip is possible. It is possible through the study of His words to us.

If our local church body is not growing, we should stop and ask ourselves, *"Are we growing in the Lord?"* We should ask ourselves, how many times in the last six months have I attempted to tell a friend, not about our church, but about what Christ has done for me and what He wants to do for them? [3]Ken Hemphill, in his book, *"The Bonsai Theory of Church Growth,"* brings to our attention that as Jesus established the church as recorded in **Matthew 16,** *The Lord Promised He would build His church.* Thus, church growth is both Natural and Supernatural. It is natural for the Church to grow and increase because it was created as a living body to grow. Secondly it should have Supernatural Growth because God has ordained and founded the Church. So according to Ken, for the church not to grow, artificial measures must be taken to keep the church from growing. Many churches work at being Bonsai churches, restricting the growth, rather than allowing that which is natural to take place.

**If I, as an individual disciple of Christ
am not sharing or attempting to share Christ,
then I am in the process of restricting the
growth of my church
and my personal spiritual growth.
Then I definitely need a trip through Hell on the
Magic Church Bus.**

The powerful soul-winner and founder of the Salvation Army, William Booth, was once asked, *"Do you think you have the best training program to teach people how to witness for Jesus Christ and win souls to Jesus?"*
William Booth replied,

"No, I don't think my methods are the best methods. I think the best method of giving people a burden for lost souls would be to take them to the devil's hell and allow them to experience what it is to be lost in hell, separated from God for an eternity in the fire that could never be quenched. Then I believe men would truly have a burden and know what it is to be soul-winners because they would see what it is to be lost."

The intent of this book is to do just that. So that the Lord might allow each of us to see and experience Hell. That we might get off our couches, and out of our Ivory towers (the church building). Then hopefully we will begin to be the church that God intended for us to be.

Lord, help us today and in the days to come, to get a real sense of your calling upon our lives. Lord, help us to see and feel Hell in all its torments and experience the wonders of Calvary on which Christ paid the price that we do not have to experience Hell. [4]*Lord, help this beggar that has found The Bread of Life, to not be greedy, but take this bread and share it as I become a fisher of men.*

Chapter 3

THE
TRAP
AT
OUR FEET

S o often we who call ourselves Christians, set a trap for ourselves. We set a trap or net that entangles our walk with Christ. This trap we set causes us to fall, and hinders others from coming to know Christ as their Lord.

We know that hunters set traps to entangle the game. But have you ever heard of the game setting traps in which they could be caught by. No you haven't, but we Christians do just that. We set traps because we become unfocused on our Lord and His goal for our life, which allows Satan to pull the trigger, and then we fall.

Lift Up Your Eyes

As we begin our trip through Hell, many are going to be surprised at what we find in Hell. First of all, so many are going to be surprised that it is a real place. More than the surprise that Hell is a real place, we are going to come to the realization that there is nothing to compare it to. Realistically, even though you may have seen Hell with your own eyes, you can still find no words by which to describe it.

Then in not being able to and pondering on how that we might describe this place of Eternal Torment, we are going to be surprised as we continue looking. We will begin to notice the activity in which we find those there are involved in. We will be surprised to notice that first of all, all eyes are lifted. **Luke 16:23: "And in Hell <u>he lifted up his eyes</u>, being in torment,......"**
(But it's now too late)

We will notice that these people continually looked to *(traps)* themselves, to their youth, to their health, to their power, to their wisdom and knowledge. People who continually looked to the world, to possessions, to jobs and to family while they were living here on earth are now looking up, to the one they should have looked to while they had opportunity.

As Christians, we all believe that Satan is continually working at destroying the Church. The strange thing about it is, Satan does not have to work too hard to achieve his desire, because we continually let ourselves become entangled in his nets. We have put our noses in the air with our eyes on the world and our personal desires. Thus we have let ourselves get tangled up in these nets that trip us up. Our desires have resulted in nets of conflicts, jealousy and power struggles that have defeated the purpose of the local church. In our personal lives we have become so wrapped up in who we are, rather than in, to whom we belong.

We need to get our, "better than you attitude" and noses out of the clouds, and lift our eyes to Him. For as they have found out in Hell, it is the Lord and only He who can pull us out of these nets that we have become entangled in. David had learned this lesson very well as he wrote; Psalm **25:15, "Mine eyes are ever toward the Lord; for He shall pluck my feet out of the net."**

<u>The Stuck-Up's</u>

As we become a separated people and enjoy the new freedom that the Lord has given us, we find ourselves becoming so heavenly minded that we are no earthly good. We get an attitude, in that we begin to think we are better than others, and it shows. As we get this attitude our heads are aimed in the right direction, because our noses are in the air, but our eyes are not following suit. We get out of touch with what we call the real world *(those who are lost, those who are still in captivity)*. Then the problem begins, and we no longer understand why others do not come to church and fellowship with us. But at the same time, the so called real world begins to wonder, where in the world our heads are, because they now feel a coldness coming from us. If we sincerely would try to recognize what is happening, we might agree, that what the church needs, *is a major attitude adjustment.*

An attitude adjustment, where we the saints, realize that the difference that is in us, is not of ourselves, but of Him. When we realize that it is His Holiness and His righteousness that makes us different and not ours, then hopefully we will begin to realize Who He is, who we are and who they are. At that moment we should understand that it is His desire that we lead the lost to Him, not drive them away with our Holier than thou attitude. Remember, we are only sinners, just as they are, but we have been saved by the grace of God, as they also can be. We need a change of attitude. Our attitude needs to become one that would begin to lead them and point them to Christ, rather than drive them away from the church.

You see our attitude not only entangles our walk and causes us to trip, but our holier than thou attitude also trips up those who need to see Jesus; they don't need to see you and me. Remember Christ said, **"And I, if I be lifted up from the earth, will draw all men unto me." John 12:32.** Another question each of us should ask ourselves,

**"In my life and in my church,
who is being lifted up?
To Whom is
worship, praise and honor
being given to?"**

Our *Attitude*, which can be sometimes defined as *Pride,* becomes a trap which begins to trip us up. We may not fall on our face because of this attitude of pride, but what so often happens is that others fall because of the trap and entanglement that we allow ourselves to get caught up in. As we learn to walk with Christ and lift Him up, we must be careful that in the process, that we don't begin to lift self.

The world considers an attitude adjustment, a slap in the face from someone else. Today, many of us need a major slap. At this point it <u>might</u> be a <u>good idea</u> to turn to a friend and ask them to, *"Slap the tare out of you."* If you did, I'm sure of one thing, you would remember reading this book. But on the other hand it may be a <u>bad idea</u>, because then we'd start bragging about being persecuted for Christ's sake. Pride would inflate us again. Instead of asking a friend to slap you, ask your Best Friend in prayer,

"Lord, I need an attitude adjustment. Please today, slap me plum silly. Slap me so that the final results will be that, you slap some common sense into me. Lord, wake me up and get my attention, because Hell is real. I'm not going there, but some

I love, are on their way. Lord I need an Attitude Adjustment"

The Sin of Being Self-centered

Discouragement is another way that we get entangled in our walk. When we take our eyes off Him, and begin to look to ourselves, when we begin to look to our achievements, our knowledge, and our wisdom, then we begin to set goals for our life and ministries that are not His. Eventually you and others will disappoint you and let you down, and then you will find yourself in *the trap of discouragement.*

Darrell Robinson in his book, "Total Church Life," gave three Priorities for pastors that could be good advice for all of us to consider. Darrell wrote, *"Some of the soundest council that could ever be given are these three things: First, preach the word. There is nothing else to preach. Second, love people - even when they don't love you and when they are unlovable. Third, keep your eyes on Jesus. You will never be disappointed. Disappointment comes when we take our eyes off Jesus and fix them on others or ourselves. Disappointment always leads to discouragement.*

Two responsibilities exist when a preacher becomes discouraged. He can repent or quit. God cannot use a discouraged preacher. When discouragement comes, the preacher is finished.

Discouragement is sin - the sin of self-centeredness. When we become discouraged, it means that we have gotten our eyes on ourselves rather than on Jesus. When discouraged, we face three alternatives: repent of the sin of discouragement, resign and move on, or quit the ministry altogether. Keep your eyes on Jesus to guard against getting disappointed or discouraged."

Again this is good advice not only for preachers, but can be applied in part to all born again believers. Instead of getting discouraged and letting Satan interfere with our walk with Christ and destroy our testimony, **we need to keep our eyes on Jesus.**

Yes, Satan is out to destroy our witness. In most of our lives he does not have too work to hard at accomplishing his goal. Because again, so many times we lay the trap, all he has to do is pull the trigger.

The Untouchables

Another way that we let ourselves become entrapped is through entanglements in this world. As we enjoy His blessings on our lives, we become more like king David, sitting in our castles rather than out on the battle field, where we should be (2 Samuel 11 & 12). In doing so we become so wrapped up in the way that we have been blessed, that we find we are spending more time enjoying His goodness, rather than sharing His Good News.

Yes, it is His will that all His children enjoy this life as we pass through. But He also has a plan for reaching the lost. That plan is you and I. God never intended for the church to be known as *"The Untouchables"*.

He would rather we had a reputation of being real people in a real world.

Where we work real jobs and live realistic survival type lives which are reaching, touching and making a difference in the lives of the people that we touch everyday.

Churches that only teach that people are reached for Christ through the preacher or by going door to door knocking, are failing to follow the example that Christ led as He witnessed. Christ showed interest in the person, He became involved in their life. We the church today, must begin to teach and practice lifestyle evangelism. Evangelism where each of us go eye to eye, and heart to heart with the ones we love and are concerned about. We demonstrate His love by investing our time in getting to know them, learning what they feel their needs are. So that we then, can share with them the real need of their life.

The Great Commission then does not stop, but continues by instructing us to continue investing our time in training them. So that they can also become lifestyle evangelists for Christ, as they also become His disciple.

As we take our trip through Hell, there is no doubt we will notice the endless dying, but never dying. We will also notice the nakedness, and the Equality of Hell. And I'm sure we will notice the pain and torment, as there is no rest in Hell. Because the fire, is a devouring, ever burning fire that cannot be quenched. We will mostly notice that there is neither love nor rejoicing there. These things will surprise many of us on this trip through Hell, as it has most of them who are now there. Again, the greatest revelation that most us would discover, if such a trip were possible, is first of all, that Hell is real, that it is eternal and that it is for ALL people who reject and neglect to allow Christ become the Lord of their life.

This same revelation is also the greatest surprise to those who are now there, for all eternity. They now realize Hell is real. That Hell is not a fairy tale or a scary story. Hell is real and it is a place for all the men and women who have rejected Christ as the Lord of their life. Hell is eternal, where those there will continue to experience dying but never dying. Hell is a place created for the Devil and His followers. If we could only see Hell as a real place, then the Church would begin to live the Great Commission.

We would not be known as
The Untouchables.

If the Church could only take a trip to Hell, we too would begin to lift our eyes and seek Him. For when we begin to seek Him and His direction for each of us, then we will find where true vision for a lost world comes from. Then we will find the power to follow and achieve great things for Him. **Isaiah 40:26, "Lift up your eyes on high, And see who has created these *things,* Who brings out their host by number; He calls them all by name, By the greatness of His might And the strength of *His* power; Not one is missing." (NKJV)**

Lifting Hands follow will Lifted Eyes

Today there is very little lifting of the hands or the voice to praise the Lord. Why you may ask? When from the front of the Bible to the back it continually says, lift your hands, lift your voices, even lift your feet and lift your eyes. The answer is, unless the eye is lifted to the Lord there is no lifting of the hands or the voice in praise. Because where our eyes are looking, is where we are headed and where our desires are. **Luke 11:34 says, "The lamp of the body is the eye. Therefore, when your eye is good, your whole body also is full of light. But when *your eye* is bad, your body also *is* full of darkness."**

The trap that we have allowed ourselves to be in trapped in, is "Pride", *Pride in the possession* of the things of this world. Our noses may be lifted as we make our way to the church house but our eyes are not focused on the Lord and who He is, but on us and who we think we are. Remember;

**"Christ must be Lord of all
or He is not Lord at all."**

Our churches according to [1]Dr. James Kennedy have become a place where we think,

**"The congregation is the audience,
the Preacher is the orator or conductor,
and God is the Performer."**

But Dr. Kennedy reminds us, the truth is;

**"The congregation is the performer
and God is the Audience."**

At the Southern Baptist Convention, at the Georgia Dome 1995, President Jim Henry, Pastor of First Baptist Orlando, made this statement. *"If there is something you are holding on to that you can't throw or give away, it owns you instead of you owning it."* When something or someone owns you, it is your lord. When we lift our eyes to look to the Lord, there ought to be nothing in our life that we would not be willing to throw away. When He is Lord, there is a commitment to live for our Lord and Savior Jesus Christ.

**When Christ is Lord of our life
we should have a desire to share
what we have in Him .**

Our Greatest Possession

For Example, take five index cards and with a pen write on each card your most prized possessions. Now imagine that God has spoken and is going to allow Satan to take everything from you, kind-a-like He did with ole Job, but He was going to allow you to keep your five most prized possessions. In other words the five things that you write on these cards are the only things that you can keep. Remember only one possession per card. If children come to your mind, you can write children on one card, there is no need to name them separately. After serious thought has been applied to your most precious possessions and you have wrote them down, think about these five possessions. Now imagine that God has decided to let Satan take one more of them away from you, but in His grace He allows you to decide which four you will keep. Now you have only four cards and basically four very treasured possessions. Please think on them for a moment.

As in the life of Job, Satan has returned to God and demands that you are only serving Him because of what He has allowed you to keep. So God allows Satan to take one more item from you, but again, He declares that you are the one who must choose which three you will keep and which you will lose. But Satan is still not satisfied that you truly love God with all your heart, so God allows him to take one other card, but again you must choose. Now that you have discarded three of your most prized possessions you only have two. How precious are these two possessions?

In the Scripture we are reminded of other great patriots of the Lord's kingdom, such as Abraham. I'm sure you remember how the Lord asked Abraham to leave his home, country and family to go to a land he didn't even know existed, or where it was. Abraham was willing to trust God for all and with everything.

Today the Lord is not asking you to give up all your precious possessions, but He does ask, of the two that you now have, if He were to take one of them away, which would you keep. After very much thought, hold on to that which is most valuable and allow the other to be discarded. Now, as you look at this wonderful possession that you hold in your hand, ask yourself the following question about this possession.

"Is this possession that you now hold?
A possession that you can truly keep?"

As you consider this question and this possession that you now hold in your hand, and as you consider this matter, think with me on this. If this most prized possession that you now hold in your hand is not Christ, The Holy Spirit, your relationship with God, or salvation which is through Christ, then in reality can you truly keep it?

This is truly a good test of our priorities and where our eyes are truly focused. This is now a good time to re-focus our eyes on Him.

In Hell, they are now lifting their eyes to the only One Who can help them, but He will not help them, because it's now too late for them. Today instead of lifting our noses, we need to lift our eyes to where our help comes from and put our noses back in the Book before we drown.

Eyes Lifted and Open

One of the great differences you would see in the church today after a trip to hell would be *our vision.* We would discover that we have allowed Satan to put blinders on each of us, the church. With these blinders on which we have allowed ourselves to begin looking to beautiful, magnificent buildings that we honor and adore, not realizing that they along with our formalities are only tools that God allows us to use. Then we would understand that any tool is suitable to be used of God. A barn, a stump, a river bank, a bar, even great cathedrals would become churches of Worship. Anywhere we could share the Good News would become a great pulpit of opportunity.

We would no longer look to formality and the way things have been done in the past, but would use formality and structure only as starting points to achieve true worship.

**Our programs for teaching, training
and reaching
would come alive with activity
as we stopped looking to ourselves
and started looking to Him.**

Lord, help us today, as we look into hell. Help us to look into ourselves. Lord as we seek your kingdom and your righteousness first. In doing so, may our eyes be opened and lifted to you, that our hearts may be burdened for the lost ones we love, and you love.

Lord, that in lifting our eyes we may become strong in you, that as you pluck our feet out of the nets and traps that we have became entangled in. That again the Church would be added to daily.

Chapter 4

CRYING IN THE CHAPEL

Luke 16:24, "Then he <u>cried</u> and said, 'Father Abraham, have mercy on me, and send Lazarus that he may dip the tip of his finger in water and cool my tongue; for I am tormented in this flame."

In Luke 16:24 we see one of the major activities in which this man in Hell is involved in. He is crying, crying for mercy, crying to see a familiar face and crying for just one drop of water.

What he asks for does not seem like much, but it's much, much more than he deserves. All his life, he had sufficient opportunity to receive the gift of eternal life that God so mercifully allowed to be purchased for him at a great price. God was willing and Christ gave His life that this man and all people might not have to experience this Hell. If in his life time, he had only humbled himself and asked, cried out to Christ to become the Lord of His life. If he had only said, *"I accept this great gift with which you have so lovingly purchased with your life."* If while he was living, he had just taken the time to cry, *"Lord, I accept!"*

But he didn't. Instead of accepting the Gift that Christ has purchased, at one point in his life he said, *"No,"* no to Christ for the last time. In Hell he has now lifted his eyes and begin to cry and will cry for eternity. God owes him no mercy, nor will he be shown any mercy. Neither will any other person who has trampled over God's love be shown any mercy.

Today, Is Your Day

If we today, had a true vision of Hell, as this man does, we would then know that God is merciful, while He is Holy and Just. Man on the other hand is sinful. A sinner, who so often lets the sin of pride stand between him and a victorious life.

It is too late to cry for mercy once you have entered Hell. Think about your life and just how fast it is passing by. **James 4:14** says, **"whereas you do not know what will happen tomorrow. For what is your life? It is even a vapor that appears for a little time and then vanishes away."** Paul reminds us in **2ⁿᵈ Corinthians** that today is the day of Salvation, we are not promised tomorrow.

As you are reading right now, if you do not know that you have Eternal Life through Jesus Christ, you should stop everything and begin at this moment to cry to a merciful God, *"have mercy on me for I am a sinner."*

1 John 5:13, "These things I have written to you who believe in the name of the Son of God, that you may know that you have eternal life,..."

In His Word, He left us the reason why we must be saved and directions on how that we can know that we have eternal life through Jesus Christ.

The Roman's Road

Romans 3:10	**"As it is written: There is none righteous, no, not one;"**
Romans 3:23,	**"for all have sinned and fall short of the glory of God."**
Romans 5:12	**"Therefore, just as through one man sin entered the world, and death through sin, and thus death spread to all men, because all sinned—"**
Romans 5:8,	**"But God demonstrates His own love toward us, in that while we were still**

sinners, Christ died for us."

Romans 6:23, "For the wages of sin is death, but the gift of God is eternal life in Christ Jesus our Lord."

Romans 10:9 & 10, "that if you confess with your mouth the Lord Jesus and believe in your heart that God has raised Him from the dead, you will be saved. For with the heart one believes unto righteousness, and with the mouth confession is made unto salvation."

Romans 10:13, "For whoever calls on the name of the Lord shall be saved."

Do you know Christ as your personal Lord and Savior?

Thawing The Ice Box

Not only do sinners need to cry out today, but we that call ourselves the church, need to begin to cry. If the Lord would allow us to see just a little bit of Hell and the crying that is now going on there, the church would not be so cold and indifferent. We would begin to hear crying coming from the chapels of worship across our land.

Someone will say; *"Crying is just an emotion, and we don't need emotionalism but a heart felt experience."* In rebuttal to that statement, I would say to you, *"If something is felt, there is always a reaction or an outward demonstration of that which is felt. Crying becomes a reaction of something that is genuinely felt. When I stump my toe I react with a yell. My yell becomes the reaction to the pain that my body felt."* The reason there has been no crying in the chapels, is because nothing has been felt of the pain in Hell.

At this point I will say I agree with the statement, *"The last thing we need in our churches today is emotionalism for the sake of emotions."* There has been way too much *wild fire,* as they called it in the old church, which is emotionalism for the sack of being emotional. Emotionalism that is brought on because of sad stories, funny jokes, or someone yelling is not real and is ineffective in reaching God or the Lost. The need today is not emotionalism, but a view of Hell that will cause us to react to what we then feel. We as Christians need to begin to see and believe that there is a place called Hell, that it is real and that it is eternal. That everyone who rejects Christ as their Lord and Savior will spend eternity in Hell, no matter what the reason or excuse they may give for rejecting Christ as their Lord.

When we realize this, hopefully we will get our noses out of the clouds as we lift our eyes, hearts and hands to Him, He will then lead us to begin to look around us. Where we will realize the reason most people who continue to say no to Christ is that, in reality, they are saying no, because of stiff, hardened, unforgiving members of the local church.

We must remember the church is to resemble Christ. Yet within the walls of the church buildings around the world you find the most hardened and unforgiving people. That is exactly why there is no crying in the chapel. Today, I'm afraid you can find a greater sense of acceptance, a warm friendly open spirit at a neighborhood bar, country club, lodge or even the local grocery store, than can be found at most local churches.

Why? Because we have lost the sense of urgency, we have lost the burden and the vision. We are too proud to forgive and forget. You see, crying, true crying, represents a sense of urgency, a sense of brokenness, a feeling of humble humiliation. All of these should be, but are not evident in the church.

As long as we remain stiff and hardened within the church, the love of Christ, which He has given to us to share, will not flow out into the world. [1]Steve Brown, recently quoted one of his friends, who said; ***"It is easier to love a dirty child than a stiff child."*** We may be dirty on the outside, but please, may we not be stiff. We must be willing to be broken with not only words of love but true acts of forgiving love.

We must allow the Ice Boxes that call themselves churches to thaw, that they might become hatcheries. Our goal is not to produce ice cubes but new born babes in Christ.

Sell Life Assurance

There was a point in my life that I sold Life Insurance. In my training, they taught us that when someone answered a question with "NO," we should not accept this "No" as meaning the person did not want what we were selling. Instead, when we received a "No" as an answer to a question we had asked, it simply meant we have not done our job well; that this "No" means this person needs more information. The proper interpretation was that I had not convinced them that my product was what they needed, and that I needed to do a better job in selling my product and its application to their life.

You will never find a successful insurance sales person who does not first of all own what he is selling. Secondly, you will not find a successful insurance sales person who does not believe that everyone has a need and an urgency to buy the products he is selling. The reason most Church members are not successful in selling Christ is, they themselves have not bought into the product and do not feel the urgency of its need.

**There is No Crying in the Chapel,
because the lost are not coming to the
realization of the urgency of their need for
Christ.**

**Which is because church members,
have not felt the urgency of the time nor the
need to sell *Life Assurance*.**

There has always been and must be an urgency about God. Joshua told the children of Israel, "**... choose for yourselves <u>this day</u> whom you will serve, whether the gods which your fathers served that were on the other side of the River, or the gods of the Amorites, in whose land you dwell. <u>But as for me and my house, we will serve the Lord.</u>" Josh 24:15.**

When the Holy Spirit begins to speak, it is urgent that we answer. There is an urgency about being saved, there's an urgency about the work of God, and there should be an urgency about our Christian walk.

The Lord is not slack concerning *His* promise, as some count slackness, but is longsuffering toward us, not willing that any should perish but that all should come to repentance.

But the day of the Lord will come as a thief in the night, in which the heavens will pass away with a great noise, and the elements will melt

with fervent heat; both the earth and the works that are in it will be burned up. 2 Peter 3:9-10

All Men Are Equal

Satan has led us to believe that crying or humbleness is a sign of weakness. So in our pride, we have built great walls in our life and in our church, walls to protect ourselves from appearing to be weak. Then in striving to be stronger we have become proud, hardened and unforgiving. Thus, we have become a stumbling block, or actually you could say we have built a wall around ourselves that will keep others out. Not just out of our life, but out of the family of God.

You see, Satan makes sure that the world, even without the help of the media, hears about all the conflict and problems within the church and within our lives. It is time that genuine heart felt crying should be the sound that is heard coming from the churches as we begin to tear down the walls that we have built. We must become aware, that no one can tear down these walls except those that have built them, for we are the only ones who know actually where the foundation for the wall is laid. The foundation must be destroyed before the wall will fall. Instead of destroying the foundation and the walls, we seem to now have the boldness to say, *"I am not hurting anyone else,"* (just like the alcoholic). Remember when one part of the body hurts, the entire body feels the pain. They say, that a person who will cry and release those inner most feelings will normally out live a person who is too proud to let others see they are human and have feelings.

The reason we do not like to cry, even though it is medicine for our soul, is because it makes us feel equal with all who have cried, thus showing our inadequacies. You see when we cry together we become equal, our pride melts away.

There are three places that all men are equal in this life.

First, we are all equal when we come to the foot of the cross. There we cry as we realize we are inadequate and deserve Hell as our eternal home. Then we continue to cry because of the joy that we then experience of knowing that Christ has loved us so much and has purchased eternal security for us at such a great price.

Secondly, we are all equal when death comes to us or someone we love. Again we realize we are powerless as we cry because of the hurt of an indefinite separation. At the grave side the ground is always level. Everyone feels the humiliation of the grave as we cry.

Third, we are all equal when we become broken, humbled and feel the urgency to forgive, or to ask for forgiveness, that we begin to release our feeling through our tears. When we are willing to be broken then we are willing that all the walls come down.

Urgency + Humbleness = Revival

For true revival to come to our world, through the church, the church must come to the point, that we see the lostness of the world. As we take a good look at ourselves, it is then that we will be able to see the dark shadows and thick walls that we have allowed to come into our churches. It's time we sense the urgency of the need, then be willing to be broken, that we may not be strong as individuals, but that the Church might be strong, in that Christ is exalted.

When we the church begin to realize that real people go to a real Hell, and that these people going to Hell are people that we know and love. Hopefully we will then begin to see the bondage that they are in. Yes, Satan has them bound in sin, yet there are those who are bound not only because of their sins, but because of our sins. We have built great walls due to our sin of pride and un-forgiveness that is blocking them from seeing Christ. Hopefully when we see people we love going toward Hell, stumbling over us, it will break us; break us to the point that we begin to cry as the children of Israel began to cry, because they could not pray. **Exodus 2:23-25,** describes what I am talking about as it says; **"Now**

it happened in the process of time that the king of Egypt died. Then the children of Israel <u>groaned</u> because of the bondage, and they <u>cried out;</u> and <u>their cry came up to God</u> because of the bondage. So <u>God heard their groaning</u>, and God remembered His covenant with Abraham, with Isaac, and with Jacob. And God looked upon the children of Israel, and God acknowledged them."

As with the children of Israel, we may not be able to pray words because of the burden of bondage which we are under, but we can cry (groan). The children of Israel began to cry because the burden of the bondage had literally become so heavy upon them. Hopefully we the church of The Living God, will begin to sense the bondage that we have allowed to come into the church, and begin to understand how that it is separating us from the power and love that we should have for the lost and our Lord, which should cause us to begin to cry out for deliverance from this great bondage.

Paul lets us know in **Philippians 3:13 & 14** that he was not going to let anything, any person or any feeling stand between him and being all that God wanted him to be. Paul said, **"Brethren, I do not count myself to have apprehended; but one thing I do, <u>forgetting</u> those things which are behind and <u>reaching forward</u> to those things which are ahead, I press toward the goal for the prize of the upward call of God in Christ Jesus."** Paul had his eyes on Christ, he was unwilling to let anything or anyone hinder or interfere with the relationship he had with Christ. So Paul was willing to forget and forgive the past, and was willing to begin to tear down all the walls and foundations that might have kept him from being the great light that God had intended him to be.

Many of you right now are beginning to think. If I am going to tear down walls in my life, which may be blocking others from seeing Christ exalted in my life, then I first must begin to forgive others and even the past. And you are thinking, now this is so hard to do and even asking how much and how often should I forgive? This is when we must come to Christ as Peter did and ask Him, rather than asking each other these questions, because He has already answered it for us when He answered Peter' question in **Matthew 18:21-22** which Peter asked, **"Lord, how often shall my brother sin against me, and I forgive him? Up to seven times?"** Jesus then said to him and us, **"I do not say to you, up to seven times, but up to seventy times seven.**

Please, Forgive Me Lord!

For some reason when we sense that we have been wronged or hurt by someone, we think that it is their place to make things right. We see it as their place to ask forgiveness. Christ taught differently and exemplified His teachings. In **Matthew 6:14 & 15,** He taught, **"For if you forgive men their trespasses,** your heavenly Father will also forgive you. **But if you do not forgive men their trespasses, neither will your Father forgive your trespasses.**" As He went to the cross He put His teachings and words into action when He said, "**Father, forgive them, for they do not know what they do.**" **Luke 23:34.** Christ forgave the soldiers at the point of offense. Christ became weak that He might be strong.

**You see if Christ had not forgiven them,
at that moment,
He would have sinned.**

With sin in His life, He would not have been able to lay His life down for the sins of others and take it up again victorious over Death, Hell and the Grave. He never would have become the Sacrificial Lamb which would reign victoriously forever. Christ forgave them, though they never asked.

**Until we are willing also to forgive,
there is an unforgiven sin in our life
that we will stand in judgment for.**

**When there is unforgiven sin in our lives,
there is a coldness and a separation between us
and God.**

**It is a battle in your life that is defeating the
effectiveness and ministry of His church.
Because of this lack of crying in the chapel,
there is crying in Hell.**

The Bible plainly teaches that before a soul can be born into the family, the family must be broken and bonded together. **"He who continually goes forth <u>weeping</u>, Bearing seed for sowing, Shall doubtless come again with <u>rejoicing</u>, Bringing his sheaves with him." Psalms 126:6.** Before sheaves and seeds, there must be a going forth and weeping. Weeping comes because of a conscious awareness of the urgency of the times in which we live, which should bring a brokenness of the proud unforgiving spirits we have adapted to in our lives.

There is no help or hope for the local church, nor for revival, until God hears crying coming from the chapels. There will be no crying in the chapel until the Church sees itself as the two blind men in **Matthew 9:27.** They saw themselves blind and helpless, but were willing to follow Christ, which began with them first looking to Him and crying out for mercy. We need to come to the place as they did then, the place where we begin to look to Him and cry aloud for mercy.

Then hopefully we will begin to pray as the father of the child that had the dumb spirit in **Mark 9:24.** He began by admitting his faith was not what it should be. He prayed and cried with a sense of urgency as we should, as we look to our heavenly Father. **"Immediately the father of the child cried out and said <u>with tears</u>, 'Lord, I believe; help my unbelief!'"** When we feel the pain, the urgency that God wants us to feel, we will then be broken. Then a real Revival can begin in each of us and in the local church.

May God hear heart felt crying coming from our chapels before others begin to cry from Hell. May the world hear crying coming from the chapels that they will sense the urgency of the times and begin to cry with us now, not later in Hell. Lord, there are many who will read these words, that have been offended by friends. They are unforgiving to those who have offended them, and that even hurts more. It hurts because they've lost through pride, what should be a victorious walk. Hurts and pride have built walls, even a fortress around them. Because of the sin that is in their life, there is a feeling of separation from you. Because of this separation they cannot worship as they once could, neither is their testimony as effective as it should be.

Not only is there the sin of being unforgiving in their life, but now there is the sin of unbelief, the feeling that this is an impossible situation. Lord, help our unbelief, as today we come crying and broken that you might again mold us together into the church and a people that will go forth from here not only with seed, but a heart felt cry that not only you can hear, but that the world can hear. That in doing so, we the church will return bringing others with us, as we rejoice.

Matthew 6:12 "And forgive us our debts, As we forgive our debtors."

Chapter 5

PRAYER
CHANGES
ME

Have you heard the story of the preacher who preached the same message every service for months? Finally, one of the church members asked him, when was he going to preach another message? He replied, *"When the church hears the one I've been preaching."* At this point it may seem that this book is very repetitious. It is, hoping that we will hear the message. Please, keep your ears and heart open to hear what the Lord would have you to hear.

You can probably say, as I can, *"I have heard about Hell all my life."* We have not only heard about Hell from the church, but you have probably heard more about it, from the world. Or at least heard the name of the place called Hell mentioned more in your none church life than in your church life. Satan likes for people to use the name of his eternal abode often, loosely and lightly. To most people, if we use a word frequently it becomes just that, another word, a word that has no real meaning. Not only has Satan lead people to use the name of Hell lightly, he has led us to the conception that the word Hell is a verb, adverb or adjective, but the truth is Hell is a noun. Hell is a real place and will not go away because we begin to think of it as an adverb. Not only have many come to think of Hell as an adverb or an adjective, but many have also come to think of God as an adverb or adjective. Many have also stopped thinking of God as a noun, which He is. We have begun to use His name in vane. God is a noun, God is God, and will be God whether or not you choose to believe in His existence. We have allowed God to become just another word with no meaning, no reverence and no power.

But there will always be power in His name. Without Him there would be nothing, not even you and I. You may say you don't believe in God or in Hell. Do you really think that will make them go away? You can also say you don't believe a 747 can fly, but it's not going to stop it from flying. Even though the word Hell may become meaningless to you, it will not make the realization of its existence go away. Because you use God as an adverb will not do away with His power over your eternal destination.

While reading the comics in the paper, which is my favorite part of the News Paper, Johnny Hart wrote one called, [1]B.C.. In one particular strip, the two men are sitting on a hill looking out over the ocean. One asks the other, *"Do you believe in Heaven and Hell?"* The other then replies, *"It depends on what I did the night before."* If most of us would be honest, that's pretty much how we all view Hell. But neither Heaven nor Hell will go away because we have a moment in which we feel it is not important to believe that they exist.

God Does Not Hear Your Prayers?

So how much should be preached or said about Hell? It should be preached about and taught about until we believe it exists and feel the pain that is coming out of it, the pain that will continue to come out of it for all eternity. I have been told that the Bible contains more about Hell than it contains about heaven. If this is true, God must have had a reason to put it that way. Maybe, the Lord put so much about Hell in His Word, which He knew His children would be reading. that we would wake up to its realization. We get so excited about going to Heaven, but a fact greater than that is, we are not going to Hell, which we deserve. Yet others may, if we don't feel the heat, and begin carrying the message of love and hope to them.

When the church begins to feel the pain that is in Hell, then we the church, hopefully will stop looking to the world and to ourselves. Start looking to Him. Begin to cry within because of the burden that we feel. Then the lines of communication will be opened, so that we then can pray as the people in hell **are now praying**,

"Father,
that you would send him
to my father's house."

We see here a couple of wonderful lessons, which seem so hard for us to learn today.

What we call praying is not necessarily praying.

Just because we think we are praying does not mean God is hearing. There is no reason to pray if God is not listening, so we must remember, God is Holy. If there is sin that you are wrestling with in your life, a sin that you know is there, but you are unwilling to deal with, a sin that you continually endeavor in, such as:

1. Idolatry: the worship of materialism.
2. Adultery: the lust of things that do not belong to you.
3. Not doing good for a neighbor when you know you should.
4. Not forgiving because someone has not asked to be forgiven.
5. Being judgmental of others, seeking always to judge and correct others rather than looking at the great sin that exist in your own life. etc.....

This is just a short list of some of the most popular sins that exist in many of our lives, which we will allow to continue to exist because we do not feel the heat of Hell and are not serious about our relationship with God.

We think of God so many times, as one would a butler or servant, thinking He is sitting on His throne with an ear in our direction waiting to meet our every need. We must realize, God does not, nor will He hear every time we think we are praying. God cannot hear you as you pray, if there is willful sin in our life. Yet, He is listening to hear us say, *"Father forgive me, because I am weak, and You are strong, my sins are many. Lord I ask, please forgive me of my sins toward You and others, as I forgive those that have sinned against me."*

Remember, Christ continually forgave the soldiers as they spit on Him, slapped His face and mocked His Holy name, by saying, ***"Father, forgive them."*** He could not have said that, if He, Himself was not willing to forgive. He desired to be sinless and was. He desired to be always able to communicate with The Father.

When the Disciples asked Christ to teach them how to pray, the prayer that He taught them included, **"And forgive us our debts, As we forgive our debtors." Matthew 6:12.** Then as soon as He finished teaching them this prayer, the first thing that He then addressed about the prayer, was forgiving others. **Matthew 6:14, "For if you forgive men their trespasses, your heavenly Father will also forgive you. 15 But if you do not forgive men their**

trespasses, neither will your Father forgive your trespasses." A simple conclusion to this thought would be, one cannot have prayers heard by a Holy God if he is holding ill feelings against another person. So before we approach God to save our lost loved ones, we must first approach each other in a spirit of love and forgiveness.

Prayer Is Two Way Communication

Prayer is not talking to God, or at God, but talking with God. Our so called prayers today have become more and more like an FM radio station. Where we become the DJ sitting behind a microphone talking to God, a one directional signal, but God is not an audience who is sitting out there eagerly waiting for us to talk at Him or to Him. All through the Bible, as you study the prayers of the Bible, you will learn that prayer is conversation. Conversation is what takes place on a telephone not a radio station, where you have two parties (persons) both with a receiver and both with a transmitter, so that after one speaks, the other can respond. Our prayers consist of us speaking, then hanging up on God when He begins to speak (**how rude!!!**) That is neither conversation nor prayer. [2]Herbert Lockyer has a tremendous book on prayers. As I studied it, one of the greatest truths that I have learned is, when God speaks, I should listen and obey. From

Adam to Paul, even Christ, when they prayed, they listened for a response from God.

It seems it would hurt God, that most of us spend more than an hour a day watching TV. *(Which now days, is neither entertaining nor informative, but is leading us into moral corruption.)* Yet, how many of us spend at least one hour a day in prayer communicating with our heavenly Father, the Lord of Lords? Think about it. We have the wonderful privilege of sitting and talking to the God of all creation and building a wonderful relationship, but we'd rather let Hollywood destroy our morals.

Why do we the church spend more time reading the daily news paper, *which if you were asked to raise your hand if you believed everything that was written in the paper to be the absolute truth, you would not raise your hand. Because none of us actually believe what the paper contains to be the absolute truth.* Yet, we will spend more time reading the paper and magazines today, than we will spend reading the Word of God. So why do we spend more time in front of a TV than we do communicating with our Lord and dearest friend? Why do we spend more time reading a paper than we do reading His letters to us? Why? Basically, we are afraid of the results. We're afraid our life will be changed. We are afraid that others may begin to look to us as they did to Christ. We're afraid that Revival will break out and that it might break out in us.

If the church is going to be the source that God uses to bring Revival throughout this World, we must begin to Pray. We find in **Acts 1:14, "These all continued with one accord in prayer and supplication..."**. Before the church had power to penetrate the world, they spent time in prayer, not only talking to Him, but listening for His response. As they prayed, they learned one of the greatest lessons we need to learn about prayer.

> *"Prayer does not change things,"*
> as we have come to believe. But,
> ***"PRAYER CHANGES ME".***

Acts 2:2-4, "And suddenly there came a sound from heaven, as a rushing mighty wind, and filled the whole house where they were setting. Then there appeared to them divided tongues, as of fire, and one set upon each of them. And they were filled with the Holy Spirit and began to speak with other tongues, as the spirit gave them utterance." As they prayed, God through their prayers began to change them, not things. The fire of the Holy Spirit began to consume them, to cleanse them and to illuminate Christ through them. The Holy Spirit through the mighty rushing wind took those flames and spread them that others might be caught up in the flame. Through these few (about 120) the world experienced true Revival. It wasn't some great program or some great speaker, but

God's people, who knew the power of prayer and were obedient to stay and pray (communicate with God) until the answer came.

They listened, received the answer and were eager to share with others. So much that it was said that they turned the World upside down. **Acts 17:6, "But when they did find them, they dragged Jason and some brethren to the rulers of the city, crying out, these who have turned the world upside down."** Think about it. From this small group that was willing to pray, the world was turned upside down. *What power!*

NO GOD, NO POWER
KNOW GOD, KNOW POWER!

Revival When?

Why is it not happening today? Why are churches splitting and dying instead of sprouting and growing? Why are there more babies being born into the world than there are children being born into the family of God? The answers to all the above questions are very simple, there is no real prayer! In **John 14:12-15** Jesus said, **"Most assuredly, I say to you, he who believes in Me, the works that I do he will do also; and greater works than these he will do, because I go to My Father. And whatever you ask in My name I will do. That the Father may be glorified in the Son. If you ask anything**

in my name, I will do it." Again we see the answer to all the questions are, "We have not prayed!" Thus we have not been changed and Christ has not been glorified.

**A so-called great service or great church
is not the results of
a talented choir,
a well trained preacher,
or even the right program.
It is the product of people that
are empowered of God,
where He is visible and abundant.**

When God's people begin to pray and wait for the response from God, then great things will happen. It's a promise from God Himself.

2Chronicles 7:14 "if My people who are called by My name will humble themselves, and pray and seek My face, and turn from their wicked ways, then I will hear from heaven, and will forgive their sin and heal their land.

It's His Promise!

Dr. James P. Gills in his book [3]"The Prayerful Spirit" quoted, [4]Leonard Ravenhill writing, *"Prayer must have priority. Prayer must be our bolt to lock up the night, our key to open the day."* He then went on to say, *"Prayer is the single most impor-tant thing we can do to know God, to be in union with Him. If we don't have a good prayer life, our priorities get mixed up."*

C.H. Spurgen, was once asked; *"Why is it that some people are often in a place of worship and yet they're not holy?"* He replied, *"It is because they neglect their (prayer) closet. They love the wheat, but they do not grind it; they would have corn, but they will not go forth into the field to gather it; the fruit hangs on the tree, but they will not pluck it; and the water flows at their feet, but they'll not stoop to drink it."*

Dr. Gills goes on to say; *"If we neglect our prayer life, we lose sight of our Lord, and we become proud and arrogant people who think we don't need God.*

Prayer, therefore, sets us straight and keeps us safe in our Lord.

How we view God and pray to Him indicates where our priorities are and whether we have the privilege of realizing that God belongs above and ahead of everything.

Prayer exerts unbelievable demands on us. As we open our hearts and allow the Lord to rule our life, He will develop us in ways far beyond anything we, on our own, have ever attempted. Worshipful prayer transcends the structure of ingrained behavior and rigid church traditions. In prayer we can experience the holy and compassionate heart of the Lord."

Psalms 18:2, "The Lord is my rock and my fortress and my deliverer; My God, my strength, in whom I will trust; My shield and the horn of my salvation, my stronghold."

When will revival come?

While we are taking our special trip through Hell we discover Revival will come;

***First, w*hen God's people begin to look to Him**
Not at each other or to each other.

***Secondly,* when we are willing to be burdened**
enough for lost souls that we begin to be broken, and tear down all the walls and gates within the church that are destroying its effectiveness, walls that have been built over many years. When we begin to cry and groan over lost victories in our lives because of sins that exist, because of unforgiving hearts.

***Thirdly,* before any other work is done,
there must be prayer,**
real prayer, prayer that is directed to the Father in reverence, recognizing His power. Prayer that is willing to wait and listen for His response.

The greatest thing that every church could do today is begin to have Prayer Meetings, (meetings where the only purpose is to pray)! The power fell when they (the church) came together in prayer. The world was shaken because the Church prayed together. God will change each of us, then the World when we begin to really pray together.

You may say, well that was 2,000 years ago; it can't happen today. But I say to that statement, according to the Bible, my God does not change, He is the same, has the same power, and has always kept His word. One great example of God working through the prayers of His people is the Brooklyn Tabernacle. Read Pastor Jim Cymbala's books, "Fresh Wind" or "Fresh Fire" and know that God moved upon Brooklyn and beyond that city, because His people met and still meet on Tuesday evenings for prayer.

The main reason lost people are not being saved is that we are not praying, and if we are praying, we are not praying for the lost. Remember the words Jesus spoke in **John 14:12-15 "Most assuredly, I say to you, he who believes in Me, the works that I do he will do also; and greater works than these he will do, because I go to My Father. And whatever you ask in My name, that I will do, that the Father may be glorified in the Son. <u>If you ask anything in My name, I will do it.</u> If you love Me, keep My commandments."** Apparently our lives and the lives of those we love are not being changed because we are not burdened about their eternal abode enough to pray and ask God to save them.

Again, there is no excuse for not spending time with God. He gives us twenty four hours each day, spend some time with Him. When we get our priorities right, there is always time for prayer.

Rest in your Father's arms

[5]Steve Brown wrote in a news letter, *"People are always asking me how to stay awake in their prayers. They will say something like, 'Steve, I simply can't stay awake. I start well but then I find myself drifting and before I know it, I'm asleep. When I wake up, I feel guilty.' Why? Guilty for sleeping on one's father's arm? Is there something wrong with that - something that is impious, something that violates the rules? If you sleep in your father's arms, you probably needed to sleep more than you needed to talk. If He needs to talk, He'll wake you up."*

The greatest reason of all that we need to spend more time with our heavenly Father is, we need His assurance, guidance and rest. And the world needs to see a living testimony that Christ is alive and reigns.

Lord, your Disciples once asked You to teach them how to pray. I know that if we were to ask You to teach us to Pray even today, You would respond to us as You did to them. I believe You would say, "When you pray, pray like this. *'Our Father which art in heaven, Hallowed be thy name. Thy kingdom come. Thy will be done in earth as it is in heaven. Give us this day our daily bread. And forgive us our sins; as we forgive those who have sinned against us. And lead us not into temptation, but deliver us from evil: For thine is the kingdom, and the power, and the glory, for ever. Amen.'"*

**Speak Lord,
as your servant waits and listens**

Chapter 6

MISSION FIELD OR MISSIONARY

As we continue our very special trip through Hell, we begin to realize that our journey is almost over. We also begin to realize that those who we have been observing, their trip will never end. As we consider those which are in Hell for all Eternity and the activities that they are involved in, we begin to notice that these people have something that we did not expect, something that so many church people seem not to have.

We have noticed that they are now looking in the right direction for their help, even though it's too late. As we hear them crying from the pain that they are feeling and listen for an answer to their prayers, we begin to realize that these Eternal residents of Hell are now **people of compassion**.

We hear and feel compassion as we read what they are crying and praying. **Luke 16:27-28**, shares with us their request of the Father **"Then he said,**

'I beg you therefore, father, that you would send him to my father's house, 'for I have five brothers, that he may testify to them, lest they also come to this place of torment.'"

We Need a Good Hard Slap - Again

Before we go any further, we need to realize that the church (the local body) has faults. We must remember not everyone in the local congregation is a saint. **Matthew 7:21, "Not everyone who says to Me, 'Lord, Lord,' shall enter the kingdom of heaven, but he who does the will of My Father in heaven."** Here we are reminded that the congregation, no matter the name on the door, the pastor nor denomination, the local church is made up of people, people that may be in leadership roles, who may not know Christ as their Lord. Then there are those who do know the Lord Jesus Christ as their personal Savior, but we are not perfect yet. We have not yet received our new body. We are sinners who have been saved by the grace of our Lord. When we realize that the local congregation is not made up of perfect individuals, then we will see the need for such a trip through Hell. Because occasionally we get so wrapped up in who we are and what we are doing that we get our eyes off the mission that we are on. <u>Occasionally we need a good slap in the face, to wake us up.</u>

(Remember the slap in chapter 2, Attitude adjustment)

Have you ever been slapped by a friend? If not, it might be a good idea to ask your best friend to slap you. Not just a friendly little pat, but to slap you plum silly. What's going to happen? You're going to feel some humility. All that pride that you have built up about your self esteem will be gone. On top of all that, if you were dozing, you're not any more. Rather than ask a friend to slap you, ask your very best friend, the Lord Jesus Christ. *"Lord, slap me plum silly, that the final results will be that you slap some common sense into me."*

Has it hit you yet that Hell is real and that in **Hell there is compassion for the Lost,** even though in Hell there is no love? **1 John 4:7-8** says **"Beloved, let us love one another, for love is of God; and everyone who loves is born of God and knows God. He who does not love does not know God, for God is love."** God will not be in Hell, so if love is of God, there is no love in Hell. But yet we see compassion in Hell. *"Lord please don't let my brothers come to this place of torment."* (Paraphrased)

So if this picture we see here is true? If you can have compassion without love, can we as the church claim to love, but yet not have compassion? The people in Hell can't love, but they sure don't want any company. They don't want you, their mother, their daddy, their brothers or sisters, or even their best friend to come to that place of torment. Maybe just maybe, if we stopped looking to heaven so much and could really feel the heat, the pain and the loneliness of Hell, we wouldn't want our mother, our daddy, our brothers, our sisters or even our friends and neighbors to go there either. We say we love God, we say we love our friends and family. We say we believe that there is literally a place prepared by the Lord for the saints called Heaven and that He has also prepared a place called Hell for Satan and all who reject Christ as their Lord. But when was the last time you shared with someone the simple plan of salvation, and told them that you loved them, but most of all that Christ loves them? If we love God as we say we do, why is it that we don't love one another enough to tell each other the truth. The Lord never asks you to invite people to church, but He commanded that we tell them about Christ and His plan of redemption for them.

At Home in My Father's House

As we have already mentioned, people have too many excuses for not going to church. But we also have just as many for not going soul winning, excuses that smell like rotten bologna. Of course if you're not supporting a local church family, you're not going soul winning. In my personal opinion, if a person does not support a local congregation with his or her presence and God's tithe, it's a very good indication that they do not have Eternal life.

**Usually when you can see a problem
on the outside,
there's a deeper problem on the inside.**

You see, since I came to the point in my life that I made Christ the Lord of my life, since I realized that I have been bought by the blood of The Lamb, my sins are washed away, and I am guaranteed a home in Heaven. There is nothing, I repeat NOTHING that can keep me from desiring to be obedient to my Lord. You see I genuinely love Him, because He loved me when I did not deserve to be loved. Because of the love I now have for Him, I have a great desire to show my love for Him. One of the greatest ways to show love to a superior person, is to be obedient to them. In His Word, He said that we were **not to forsake the assembling of ourselves together, as is the manner of some, but that we were to exhort one another, and so much the more as you see the Day approaching**" (Hebrews 10:25 Paraphrased). To make it simple for simple minds like mine, He is saying, if we are His children, then we are to come together and exhort each other. In Matthew 28:18-20, He commanded that we teach and baptize all nations. This is what we call the Great Commission, because it was not a suggestion or a request, but an order. In what other facility or organization can I follow through His orders, other than through the Church that He gave His life for.

**Because I love Him,
Because of His order,
Because He commissioned the Church,
I will attend it.**

You may keep me out of certain buildings, but you will never stop me from coming together with other believers to exhort, teach and baptize.

If someone or something can keep you from God's house, *YOU NEED TO GET SAVED!* You see I don't go to church for the preacher to shake my hand. Personally I don't care if he does or doesn't. I don't go to church because I like the choir, the preacher or the person sitting in front of me. I don't go to church to get the latest gossip or to spread it. I don't go to church because I was invited. In reality, I don't care if I'm invited or not. The purpose for going to church is to assemble with other believers who love my Lord as I do, because He said I should. I have a desire to be with Him, to get more aquatinted with Him, and to be with others who have that same desire.

Paul put it like this; **"Who shall separate us from the love of Christ? [Shall] tribulation, or distress, or persecution, or famine, or nakedness, or peril, or sword? As it is written: 'For Your sake we are killed all day long; We are accounted** as sheep for the slaughter.' Yet in all these things we are more than conquerors through Him who loved us. For I am persuaded that neither death nor life, nor angels nor principalities nor powers, nor things present nor things to come, nor height nor depth, nor any other created thing, shall be able to separate us from the love of God which is in Christ Jesus our Lord." Romans 8:35-39.** As Paul says there is nothing that can separate me from the love of my God. Why should I allow a man, woman, group or organization stand in my way of being all that God wants me to be. The scripture teaches that He wants us to come together to exhort each other, to teach and to baptize believers. Because of my love for Him, that's what I will do.

When a church member says, I don't go to church because I don't feel like I belong. That's a very good sign they don't and need to be born again.

**Because as a son
I always feel at home in my father's house
and I never have to be invited.
It's my Father's house.**

Me a Missionary?

Christ goes further and not only says, come together. He commanded that we **"...Go into all the world and preach the gospel to every creature."** Mark 16:15.** So again, if I am saved, the love of God then dwells in me and I will tell (preach) the

Good News to everyone and anybody. If I don't, I need to go back to the altar. There I need to begin to be broken, so that God then will take the broken vessel that I have placed at His feet, and mold me into a vessel of useful service.

You see in Hell they believe in Missions, about the same as most church members. He said, *"...send him..."* So many today are saying send someone. But we are not looking at who could have the greatest effect on our friends and family.

The plain simple truth is, either you are a missionary working to bring others to Christ or you are the mission field. This is a good place to STOP and THINK.

Do I believe in Mission work?

(Mission work meaning: sharing the love of Christ, The Good News, with others.)

They believe in Mission Work in Hell.

The Bible teaches and commands that God's children should tell the Good News.

So if I am not telling?

If I have not brought someone or attempted to bring someone to Christ,

Then I am not a Missionary,

Therefore I must be a Mission Field.

If you have come to the conclusion that you are not a Missionary, please STOP and PRAY, now. *"Lord send one of Your Missionaries to me, that they might introduce me to you and the Good News of the Gospel. That I might then become one of Your witnessing Missionaries."*

You may now ask the question, why do I want to be one of His Missionaries? The answer again is very simple; all God's children are Missionaries.

The only difference in a Missionary who has left his home to go to a foreign country to tell The Good News, and you is that you get to go home more often. If you are a child of God, you have been ordained by Him to be a Missionary. You are to represent your Father wherever you are.

There are so many ways to serve the Lord on your mission field. It starts by using the spiritual gifts that God has given you. Every Christian needs to know their spiritual gift. One of the easiest ways to realize your spiritual gifts is to read Larry Gilberts' book [1]"Team Ministry" and take [2]"The Spiritual Gifts" test put out by "The Church Growth Institution" or others that are published at this time.

When we know our spiritual gifts, then we realize we have a wonderful part in sharing this wonderful gift that God has given us. We all have different ways of sharing, because it takes different approaches for different folks. **Jude 1:21- 23** tells us to, **"keep yourselves in the love of God, looking for the mercy of our Lord Jesus Christ unto eternal life. And on some have compassion, making a distinction; but others save with fear, pulling them out**

of the fire, hating even the garment defiled by the flesh."

Did you notice what was said there in Jude? **"hating even the garments spotted by the flesh."** It sounds as though he has just told you and I, *you don't have to like the people, the way they dress or even approve of their ways, you've just got to love them.* (Paraphrased)

Two of the greatest opportunities that I have learned about since being saved through the redemption plan of God are, first, I don't have to spend eternity in Hell, which I deserve. Secondly, this gift that I have received is sharable, and should and must be shared, shared with those you love and those who you hate their outward appearance or ways.

It must be shared.
Remember
Someone shared it with you.
<u>**Clean The Pool**</u>

It is amazing. We get all excited when things go well, when it seems our prayers are being answered. But let the Lord begin to ask us to labor, WOW, what a roar we hear! We forget, a great harvest only comes after a season of hard work in the field. For a supportive story that is as up to date as yesterday's headlines, notice the Children of Israel and their actions in Exodus. **Exodus 4:29-31, "Then Moses and Aaron went and gathered together all the**

elders of the children of Israel. And Aaron spoke all the words which the Lord had spoken to Moses. Then he did the signs in the sight of the people. So the people believed; and when they heard that the Lord had visited the children of Israel and that He had looked on their affliction, then they bowed their heads and worshipped." When God was doing wonders they worshipped. Then notice in **Exodus 5:20-21,** after Moses and Aaron had been to see the Pharaoh, Pharaoh made the announcement that he did not know the Lord or even who the Lord was, and added to their burden. While the Children of Israel waited on God to do things His way, they had to carry a larger and heavier load. When the burden got heavy, they stopped worshipping and started complaining, and even was ready to hang the servant of God. **"Then, as they came out from Pharaoh, they met Moses and Aaron who stood there to meet them. And they said to them, 'Let the Lord look on you and judge, because you have made us abhorrent in the sight of Pharaoh and in the sight of his servants, to put a sword in their hand to kill us.'"** In other words, like so many today, they wanted to play in the kitchen, but they couldn't take the heat. A modern version of this would be, *they wanted to swim in a clean pool, but they didn't want to do the cleaning, only the playing.* We like to play like Christians, but we don't like to do the work of Christ.

Now, to clarify an earlier statement, where I said, "In my opinion if a church member does not attend church they need to get saved," I hope you did not come to the conclusion that you think that I believe that everyone that comes to church is saved. Because, I seem to agree with the statement that has been made by many including Billy Graham, "That probably 80% of the Sunday Morning crowds in our churches are lost." Because you attend church one time or ten times a week does not save one's soul, it simply means you are trying to learn or trying to get infected.

When we, the church (the local body) begin to Love God, when we make Him Lord of All; Sunday School Attendance will double, Sunday Evening Bible Studies and Evening Worship Services will triple, because His children would have a great hunger to know about Him and His Word. Midweek prayer meetings would explode, because His children would have a desire to spend hours praying together and communicating with Him. Weekly evangelism efforts would be awesome, as His family would have a great desire and hunger to learn how and begin to share this most precious gift with others.

**Genuine Love for Christ
will be reflected to the world
as Compassion for lost Souls**

To That One, I Made A Difference

The Most common excuses for not witnessing are; "It will not make a difference", "People are just too hard today", "There is no hope for them". To you that would say such things, your problem is, you don't believe in God. You actually need a trip through Hell. Because in Hell, they believe Hell is real, they believe the Bible is The Word of God, and they believe He is Divine and has Divine Power.

In Hell
They believe that He can actually
raise the dead.
BUT DO YOU?

Luke 16:30-31 says "And he said, 'No, father Abraham; but if one goes to them from the dead, they will repent.' "But he said to him, 'If they do not hear Moses and the prophets, neither will they be persuaded though one rise from the dead.' "

If we believe as we claim to believe, why don't we act like it? Why don't we live like it? The awful truth is we actually don't believe that God can take a sinner who is wrenched in sin and bring him to life in Christ, or we would spend more time crying, praying and telling. The real question that should be asked is, "Do you believe God can raise the dead?"

**We say that we believe that Lazarus and
Jesus rose from the physical dead.
So why can't we believe
that He can also bring to life
those who are spiritually dead?**

He can, I know from experience; He has given me
life and according to the scriptures we are all equally
dead or lost until Christ saves us. If He can save me,
and He did, He can also save you and anyone you
know. There is no one so spiritually dead that He
cannot give them life also.

Derric Johnson wrote in His book [3]"Easy Doesn't
Do It". *"It is one thing to have Compassion, but
another to have a Burden."* You see in Hell they
have Compassion, but they don't have Love. **1John
4:7-8** says, **"Beloved, let us love one another, for
love is of God; and everyone who loves is born of
God and knows God. He who does not love does
not know God, for God is love."** When we take the
Love of God and add compassion, we come up with
a GREAT BURDEN for the Lost. A BURDEN that
will make a DIFFERENCE!

Derric Johnson went on to say;

96

**"It is one thing to be Saved,
but another to be Surrendered.
It is one thing to be Converted,
but another to be Consecrated.
It is one thing to have The Spirit Dormant,
but another to have The Spirit Dominant.
It is one thing to have the Holy Spirit
as a resident,
but totally another thing to have
The Holy Spirit as President."**

Matthew 9:37-38 reads, **"Then He said to His disciples, 'The harvest truly is plentiful, but the laborers are few. Therefore pray the Lord of the harvest to send out laborers into His harvest.'"** Then in **Matthew 10,** He sent the Disciples out with Power to reap the harvest.

**You may say,
can I actually make a difference?
Yes,
God and You can do all things.**

It's a Promise!

Have you heard the story of the man who traveled to the Gulf for a visit?[4] As he was walking along the beach, he saw a stranger picking up Star Fish and throwing them back into the water, one by one. He asked the stranger what he was doing. The stranger explained how that it was low tide and that the Star Fish had landed on the beach and would die. So he was rescuing them. The man then thought, spoke up and said, "Don't you realize there are thousands of Star Fish on this beach and even more and more on all the beaches around the world? You alone cannot make a difference to all of them." But the stranger picked up one more and threw it back into the ocean, and then said, "To that one, I made a difference."

Until we begin to evangelize with compassion and tell others about Christ, our prayers have no legs.

**Everyone of us can make a difference
One person at a time!**

Love + Compassion = Burden

Lord, Thank you for loving me! Thank you for sending one of your missionaries to my field that they would tell me the Good News. There are so many today who claim to be Your Disciples, but yet they have never introduced anyone to You. Lord help us to feel the hurt, the pain, the loneliness and the eternal separation of Hell. That we might believe, not only that there is a Hell, but that You are God, and that You can and will raise the dead, even those who are dead in sin. Ephesians 2:1 says; "and you He made alive, who were dead in trespasses and sins".

Lord, You instructed Your Disciples to pray that the Lord of the harvest would send fourth laborers into His harvest. Lord I pray today, send laborers into your harvest, for the fields are ripe and ready but there are so few to labor. Lord, please send me. Give me the courage that I will need to go and the wisdom to know we must win them, one by one.

Chapter 7

CHECK
YOUR
BEEPER

Volunteer Fire Fighters wear a beeper or pager. If you are one, or know of a Volunteer Fire fighter, you have probably noticed that they have their beepers with them all the time. Even if something come across their pager that is not in their area, they usually go to offer their assistance if needed.

There are many professions where beepers are required to be worn by the employees. These people usually consider the beeper an irritation and troublesome. On the other hand I have never heard a Volunteer Fire Fighter complain about his beeper. The reason that you will not hear a fire fighter complain about his beeper is because he has a desire to try to help others who are hurting. He realizes that he may be the only one who can save those who are being burned out of their livelihood.

The Lord has also given His church beepers (compassion and love for lost souls). The problem is, so many have laid them down or turned the volume off. If you haven't heard yours sound out an alarm that says, "**Lost person going to Hell, They need your help**" **lately;** it's time to check your beeper.

D.L. Moody had a beeper, and was not ashamed of it. He said that on the forehead of every person he met was a large "L". Thus he considered them lost until they shared with him their experience of salvation. Some of you may think, "Well who do you think you are, God that everyone has to tell you their experience of salvation?" No, and that's exactly the reason. God knows who belongs to Him. But unless I as a Christian share with everyone that Christ has come to save them from Satan's Hell, then I do not have the compassion and love for them that a Christian should have.

Others say, I'm afraid that I will offend people if I ask them if they are saved. If they become offended, that's a very good sign that they are lost. You see, it thrills me for someone to ask me about my experience and relationship with my Lord. He has saved me from this Hell that we have been talking about, and has given me the opportunity to share this wonderful gift with as many as I can. To me it is a joy to be able to see the "L"s come off their foreheads. It is even more thrilling to hear those who have known Him for a while share how they came to know Him and to hear about their walk and relationship with Him since that day. Those who know Christ personally are always proud to introduce their Dearest Friend to others.

If after a trip through Hell and your Beeper is not blasting, you definitely need a spiritual check up. Just as the Volunteer Fire Fighter, you may be just the one who could reach them and pull them out of the Eternal Fire of Hell.

Fiction or Fact?

As we near the end of our trip through Hell on our Magic Church Bus, hopefully there is a sense of awakening spirit in your soul. The big problem is you could say that this book is a book of fiction. The Bible does not record for us that anyone ever went to Hell and returned. We know that Jesus did raise several from the dead, but it is never said that He brought any out of Hell. The Lord did give us His Word, The Bible, which tells us so much about Hell. Even though there is no magic Church Bus and we cannot go to Hell to wake up our sleeping, carefree, formal churches, we can go to the Bible.

We must first come to the realization that it is the church that needs to Wake-up, not the world.

When the church begins to read the Word of God and feel the pain and eternal separation of Hell, there will be a real Revival throughout the World. The World will then witness The Church being the Light that it should have been all the time. When we begin to read and realize Hell is real, we will then realize that the exciting thing about being a Christian is not going to Heaven, but that the most exciting thing about being a sinner that has been saved by the Grace of God is that I'm not going to Hell, which I deserve. When we realize this, then the church will fall to her knees, where we need to be. Have you heard? The way to get a church to stand is to get her on her knees.

As we have read about this place that was only prepared for the Devil and those that follow him, first of all, hopefully, we realize Hell is a real place of eternal torment and separation from all that is good.

Secondly, those who follow Satan are those who are not following Christ.

"Now by this we know that we know Him, if we keep His commandments. He who says, "I know Him," and does not keep His commandments, is a liar, and the truth is not in him."1 John 2:3-4. There are only two ways, either you are born of the Spirit bought by the blood of Christ and growing daily in Him, or you are lost and going to spend eternity in Hell. So if I do not have a desire to worship my Lord and assemble with the family of God to edify the body of Christ, I need to receive Christ as my Lord. Too often we make excuses and accept them. It is time that we realize it does not matter to the Lord whether or not the church or the Pastor accepts your excuse. He knows the heart and has stated it very clearly in **First John.** I may claim to be a Christian and not attend the assembling of the body, but the truth is a Christian will assemble as the Lord commanded. You may claim to be a Christian homosexual. Yes, God does and will save a homosexual as He will save any sinner who turns to Him and makes Him Lord. According to **Romans 1: 18-32,** you can be a homosexual who becomes a Christian, but once you become a Christian, your desire is then to please Him and be like Him, so He changes your desires. Just as He goes on and says in **Romans 1**, those who continually commit murder, fornication, gossip, cheat, lie and continually boast of their deeds, can be saved. Oh, you claim to be Christian, but your actions speak louder than your words. He said not everyone who says unto me Lord, Lord, shall enter into the Kingdom of God. Be assured that God can save and rescue all persons from the eternal death of Hell. When He does, they become a new person in Christ. That's why we are called Christian, because our life should resemble that of Christ Himself. **Romans 1:29-30,** also speaks of those who stir up strife, those who are untrusting, unforgiving, un-loving and unmerciful. Yes, all these can be saved, but saved persons will not practice these things.

Thirdly, if I do not love there is a serious problem.

1John 2:9-11, "He who says he is in the light, and hates his brother, is in darkness until now. He who loves his brother abides in the light, and there is no cause for stumbling in him. But he who hates his brother is in darkness and walks in darkness, and does not know where he is going, because the darkness has blinded his eyes." A Christian cannot be prejudice toward others. If we do not have a great burden (love) for all mankind, we are not walking the walk, as He tells us in **First John 2:6.** For when we walk in the light as He is in the light, we will find God's people taking seriously the work of the kingdom. And that work is to, "GO TO ALL THE WORLD, MAKING DISCIPLES."

Please Notice, Please, Please Notice! Yes, in Hell it seems the people there are doing what we the church should be doing. They are looking up; their eyes are lifted as ours should be. They are crying and willing to be broken, while we are being trapped. They are praying and listening for an answer, and they have great compassion for you and me that we don't join them. But they have no opportunity nor will they ever have another opportunity to be saved. We do not know where this man lived while he was living, nor do we know what kind of business he may have been in. We do not know which synagogue he attended or if he attended. But what we do know, he never accepted God as his Lord of all. In not making Him Lord we know that he was not a follower of God but a follower of Satan. Thus, he will spend eternity experiencing eternal death.

Because he made this decision to follow Satan during his life here on earth, he now has no opportunity to warn his brothers and sisters or friends about the place where he is.

Because his decision not to live for God while he lived, but to live for himself and the things of this world which will pass away, he no longer is living, but dying for eternity. **1John 2:15-17** says, **"Do not love the world or the things in the world. If anyone loves the world, the love of the Father is not in him. For all that is in the world—the lust of the flesh, the lust of the eyes, and the pride of life—is not of the Father but is of the world. And the world is passing away, and the lust of it; but he who does the will of God abides forever."** Think about it. God was so good to this man to allow him to enjoy the wonderful things of this life that God created for His children to enjoy.

God has allowed you and me to breathe and enjoy this beautiful world which He created. He has also given you and I the opportunity not only to enjoy life, but to enjoy it to its fullest by allowing Him to be the Lord of our life, and live according to His plan. But where are you? And where are you headed for eternity?

1 John 5:13 says, **"These things I have written to you who believe in the name of the Son of God, that you may know that you have eternal life, and that you may continue to believe in the name of the Son of God."** Do you know Him? Does your life show evidence of Him abiding in you? If not, you have an opportunity today. Christ said in, **John 10:10, ".... I have come that they may have life, and that they may have it more abundantly."** But you must make the decision while you have the opportunity. **Acts 3:19** says, **"Repent therefore and be converted, that your sins may be blotted out, so that times of refreshing may come from the presence of the Lord,"** and **Ephesians 2:8** says, **"For by grace you have been saved through faith, and that not of yourselves; it is the gift of God".** Saved from what? Eternal death in Hell! Would you surrender to Him as Lord of your life? You can because **Romans 10:9-10** says, **"that if you confess with your mouth the Lord Jesus and believe in your heart that God has raised Him from the dead, you will be saved. For with the heart one believes unto righteousness, and with the mouth confession is made unto salvation."**

If you have never met Christ, may I introduce you to Him? Because once you arrive in Hell, there is no way out, you will die with your master (Satan) for eternity. But, if you would be broken today, and pray from your heart, **"Lord, I am a sinner, a sinner that deserves Hell. Lord, you said in your word"**

(John 3:16) 'that you loved me so much that you gave your only son, and that if I believe I could have eternal life.' Lord I believe and claim your son and His righteousness. Please come into my life. I give you total control of all that I am. I can not live the life I should alone, but with you I can do all things."

There are still many church members who need to pray this prayer. You have never witnessed for Christ, because you have no testimony. Remember He said, "You are either for me or against me". You are either a missionary or a mission field. There is no excuse for a Christian to live a defeated life. There are too many who have never heard. Christ has died on the cruel cross to give you eternal life. The least you could do is to live for Him.

THE CHRISTIAN'S PLEDGE

1. I will do more than belong; I will participate.
2. I will do more than care; I will help.
3. I will do more than believe; I will practice.
4. I will do more than be fair; I will be kind.
5. I will do more than forgive; I will work.
6. I will do more than earn; I will enrich.
7. I will do more than teach; I will inspire.
8. I will do more than give; I will serve.
9. I will do more than live; I will grow.
10. I will do more than be friendly; I will be a friend!

Church, Go To Hell, Please. That we might wake up and be about the Father's work. He left us as His stewards. We could never repay Him for Eternal Life and the great price that He paid that we may have it. But we can Love Him, and the greatest way to prove our Love is to be obedient to His command. Tell somebody about Him.

**MY DEAREST FRIEND.
YOUR DEAREST FRIEND.**

Chapter 8

LIGHT
THE
WAY

If we who are bought by the blood of Christ surrendered to His Lordship in our lives, were able to take such a trip through Hell, yes, there would be a great change in most churches. I believe many of the changes that would be noticed would include;

Music

Our Music programs would have a fresh new enthusiasm about it as our leaders lead us to Worship our Wonderful Lord and Savior who has made it possible that we may never see Hell.

Preaching

Preachers would once again get back to preaching **"Thus saith the Lord."** As they preached the Word of God, they would again not only preach with enthusiasm but with a burning desire that Christ, not man, would be exalted through their preaching. They once again would begin to preach with Power of the

Holy Spirit, because in their trip through Hell, they would have realized they need to spend more time with Him and less time socializing and catering to the world. Preachers after a trip through Hell would again realize knowledge is good, but the wisdom that comes from being with God is far better. We would begin to preach with love and out of love. After seeing Hell we would preach out of a love for our Redeemer Who has made it possible that we are not going to Hell. We again would feel honored to be called a servant of our Lord. We would preach with love and compassion for those unto which the Lord has called us to minister to. After a trip through Hell, ministers would feel the heartbeat of what Paul was saying to Timothy in **Second Timothy 4:2** and it would be exemplified in our preaching. **"Preach the word; be instant in season, out of season; reprove, rebuke, exhort with all long-suffering and doctrine."**

Teachers

If our teachers could just feel the Realization of Hell, they would understand the awesome responsibility that they have to equip the saints to make a difference in the world that is going to Hell.

Teachers, as the Preachers, would realize there is more to teaching than reading the Quarterly. The Word must be taught, taught from a genuine relationship with God Himself, and you don't get that by reading the Quarterly thirty minutes on Saturday evening. Teachers would realize Sunday School Material is good for giving a direction to study that everyone will be together, but it was not designed to take the place of God's Word. After a trip through Hell, a Sunday school teacher would take the Quarterly, read it, get some direction, and then teach **"Thus saith the Word"** from a heart that is enthused about God because they have been with Him.

Deacons

After a trip through Hell, Deacons would realize that being a Deacon in God's house is not a position of authority or administration. But a Deacon is just as the Pastor, a Servant to Servants, His church, to serve the Greatest Servant of All, Christ Jesus our Lord. After a trip through Hell there would be no more deacon meetings to discuss the business of the church, the pastor or the community. But Deacon Meetings would consist of praying and lifting each other up before the Lord as they minister to the needs within the family of the church. Deacons meetings would not consist of talking about the elderly, the youth or the problems in the church, but talking to God about the needs of ministry. Then asking how those needs should be met and then following through. After a trip through Hell, Deacons would serve with enthusiasm and encourage their pastor to spend more time with God and His Word, while they serve the tables of the church, that he as the under-shepherd would have Fresh Food for the flock to feed them by which they all could grow as he enters the pulpit.

Let the World Go to Hell

After we take our journey through Hell, after we have felt the heat and seen the pain, the hurt, the agony and the stench of endless death, we would begin to look up, we should begin to have compassion, because of the compassion that we would feel. We would begin to cry and pray. In our humiliation we would find ourselves back at Calvary where we would see the Lamb of God who died a cruel death to purchase our salvation that we would not have to spend eternity in this Hell.

As has been stated earlier, if God would allow His disciples who are living today to take such a trip, there would be Revival throughout the World? The sad fact is, He will allow it, if we would only open His Word, and allow Him to open our ears, our minds, and our hearts. But it seems, we are afraid of Revival, we're afraid of what it will cost us, and we're afraid of the change that it will bring in our lives personally. So instead of allowing, "The Church To Go To Hell," we're content with allowing the World To Go To Hell.

Lord I come to you, to present myself to you, as an unworthy vessel, but the vessel that am I, that you may take me, fill me and use me that others may see You in me. And in all things Your Name, Your Power and Your Work may be glorified.

Philippians 3:7-14 "But what things were gain to me, these I have counted loss for Christ. Yet indeed I also count all things loss for the excellence of the knowledge of Christ Jesus my Lord, for whom I have suffered the loss of all things, and count them as rubbish, that I may gain Christ and be found in Him, not having my own righteousness, which is from the law, but that which is through faith in Christ, the righteousness which is from God by faith; that I may know Him and the power of His resurrection, and the fellowship of His sufferings, being conformed to His death, if, by any means, I may attain to the resurrection from the dead.

Not that I have already attained, or am already perfected; but I press on, that I may lay hold of that for which Christ Jesus has also laid hold of me. Brethren, I do not count myself to have apprehended; but one thing I do, forgetting those things which are behind and reaching forward to those things which are ahead, <u>I press toward the goal for the prize of the upward call of God in Christ Jesus.</u>"

Foot Notes

Every effort has been made to give complete bibliographic information for all references. If the reader desires more specific information regarding any source, he or she should contact the author.

Chapter 2: A Special Trip
1. The Magic School Bus, The Public TV Network.
2. Proclaim Magazine, January-March 1995, page 9, The Task of Soul Winning.
3. The Bonsai Theory of Church Growth, Ken Hemphill, Broadman Press, Nashville TN.
4. D.T. Niles's definition of Evangelism, "It is one beggar telling another beggar where to get food," Introduction to Evangelism, Delos Miles, page 37, Broadman Press, Nashville Tenn.

Chapter 3: The Trap at Our Feet
1. Dr. James Kennedy, Author & Pastor, Coral Ridge Presbyterian Church, Coral Ridge FL.

Chapter 4: Crying in the Chapel
1. Steve Brown, Bible Teacher, Key Life Network, PO. Box 94-5000, Manitland, Florida 32794-5000. Tape Ministry, Study of Job #41

Chapter 5: Praying Changes Me

1. B.C. By Johnny Hart; 1995 Creations Syndicated, Inc. 9-9
2. All the PRAYERS of the Bible, Herbert Lockyer, Zondervan Publishing House, Grand Rapid Michigan, Copy Right 1959
3. "The Prayerful Spirit", Dr. James P. Gills, M.D., Love Press, St. Luke's Building, PO. Box 5000, Tarpon Springs, FL 34688-5000.
4. "Revival Praying", Leonard Ravenhill , Bethany House Publishers, Minneapolis, MN.
5. "Steve's Letter" Key Life Network, September 1995, PO. Box 945000, Maitland, Florida 32794-5000

Chapter 6: Mission Field or Missionary

1. "Team Ministry", Larry Gilbert, The Church Growth Institute, PO. Box 4404, Lynchburg, VA 24502
2. "The Spirtual Gift Test", The Church Growth Institute, P.O. Box 4404, Lynchburg, Va. 24502
3. Easy Doesn't Do It, Derric Johnson, Y.E.S.S. Press
4. One at a Time, Chicken Soup for the Soul, Jack Canfield and Mark Victor Hansen, Health Communications, Inc. Deerfield Beach, Florida.

THE BEST OF
FROM THE HEART

The Lord has allowed me to meet many people who have influenced and changed my life because they where special people that God sent my way, in order to help me be more of what he wanted me to be. In 1997, Ann Knight, the Editor for the Cook County News in Adel Georgia approached me with a question. She said "she felt the paper had need of someone to write an editorial with a Christian slant, and she felt the Lord had sent her to me." So she asked, if I would begin to write a weekly editorial and submit it to her to be published. Since the Lord had been dealing with me about writing three books already, and I had just finished the first draft of "Church, Go to Hell, Please" I told her that I would pray about it, and that is what I did. I prayed and then sit down and began to write, before I knew it I had written four, which I began to submit to her every week. Years later I moved to Florida and the Washington County New in Chipley and The Advertiser in Bonifay began to publish them each week also, and then other papers from time to time would pick them up from the internet and publish them. So to make a long story short, since 1997 I have been writing at least fifty editorials per year.

As I began to share with readers of the articles that I was in the process of publishing a book, several suggested that I ought to publish a book of these editorials. But what I decided for the time is ad 53 of some of my favorites of these articles/editorials to my first book and pray that the Lord would use these articles once again to be a blessing to you. Please let me know by e-mailing me at timhall_2000@yahoo.com or by going to my web page and leaving me a message there. Thank you so much, may you and yours be blessed as we adore the Lord Jesus Christ.

Hell is about Love

L et me get your opinion on a situation. There is a man and a woman, they have been friends for sometime now; they often go out together. One day he asks her to marry him because he says he loves her. But she answers, "I respect you. I admire you, but I don't love you and I don't want to marry you." Now imagine that he proposes to her a 2nd time and she declines again. And a 3rd time she declines. Finally, the man says, "You know what? I love you so much I am going to force you to marry me. I am going to force you to spend all of your life with me." Now my question is; would you consider that true love?

Well, we live in a culture today where many people basically say they don't believe in hell. They use the word a lot in their vocabulary, but say they don't believe it is an actual place. They will tell you that if there were a place, as described in the Bible, that a loving God would not send people there.

What these people don't understand is, God does not send anyone to hell, but because He loves them He allows them to choose. The first thing one must understand about God is that God does not just love, He is love. He is the definition of love. God is a loving God, but He does not love in the sense that most people use that word today, meaning a sentimental emotion, some warm fuzzy feeling that is tolerant of everything and everybody. God is a loving God, BUT - His love is a holy love. His love is a righteous love. His love is a just love. Actually because He is Love according to Ezekiel 33:11 and 2nd Peter 3:9, God does not want anyone to go to hell. It is actually a place that He created for the Devil and his angels according to Matthew 25:40.

Another thing that most people don't know or want to forget is that Jesus Christ Himself spoke more on the subject of hell than any other subject. The question is; why would He do that? Because He wanted everyone to know that it was a real place, that God gives sinners an opportunity to choose to spend their eternity there or in Heaven, a place He has prepared for them. You see, that is real love. Because the real question people should ask today is "Why would a loving God force a person to go to Heaven?" The Bible is very clear, God hates hell and He hates people going there. But God's love is so merciful and so real, that He allows people to choose hell if that is what they want.

We all know this world is filled with people who reject God's love every day, who have no desire to worship God's Son, who have no hunger to hear God's Word or fellowship with God's people. God understands that they would be totally out of place in heaven.

Can you imagine people who have had no time for God, no desire for God, no hunger for God, can't stand the thought of going to church and learning about God or hearing the Word of God, dying and ending up in heaven in an eternal church service, where 12:00 never comes, and you never get out? And spending all that time with people who do love God and are praising God and worshipping the God that they never knew and never cared for? In that sense, heaven would be hell for them.

So in a real sense, God's love demands a hell, because hell is about love. It is God loving a person so much that He gives them that which they sought and desired their entire life, a place where there is no God, a place where they will never be confronted by His love for them or about truth and what is morally right.

People also often ask why there is so much evil on the earth? The answer is the same, God created us with the ability to choose. If you believe that a human being has the right to choose and the ability to choose, then that demands that you believe in hell, for without hell, there is no choice, and without choice, heaven would not be heaven. In the real sense of the word, Heaven in reality would be hell. If your choice is only limited to loving God whether you want to or not, and going to heaven whether you want to or not, then there really is no choice at all. Hell is not simply a sentence that God passes on sinners who reject Him; it is the end of a path that is freely chosen in this life (here and now) day by day.

To every person on earth who kept God at arm's length, who has said by their actions, their thoughts,

"We don't want any part of God or any part of His son, no part of His salvation, no part of praising Him or worshiping, just want to keep Him at a distance," God says, "You want distance? I will give you the ultimate distance. I will give you an eternity totally separated from Me." It is simply the eternal fruit of an earthly life that was lived totally apart from God. But no one has to go there.

The story is told of a man sitting in a restaurant reading his Bible, when he heard two men arguing at the next table. One of the men got up to leave and as he left he said to the other "Go to Hell!" With that the man sitting in the next booth reading and listening, turned around and tapped the man on the shoulder that was left sitting and said, "I've been reading the directions and you don't have to go, if you don't want to."

No one has to go, but everyone must decide for themselves and make preparations for eternity in this life. "For God so loved the world, that he gave his only begotten Son, that whosoever believeth in him should not perish, but have everlasting life. For God sent not his Son into the world to condemn the world; but that the world through him might be saved" (John 3:16-17 KJV). What do you choose? Does your life reflect your choice?

To Fly Like an Eagle

The first things that people notice, as they walk in my office, are the Eagles. You see there are Eagle statuettes from two inches high to two feet tall. There are Eagle cups, Eagle plates, an Eagle lamp and pictures of Eagles all around the room. One of these pictures stands 3' by 5' and screams to be noticed. I even wear a tie that has Eagles all over it. It's not that I like any particular sports team or just the American Eagle Symbol. You see, all these Eagles are gifts from family and friends, because I claimed Isaiah 40:31 as my life verse early in my ministry.

You probably don't know, but I'll confess, I was one of those hyperactive children, and am a hyperactive adult. Soon after I became a young adult I could not understand why all adults were not hyperactive, and honestly I still question it at times. I'm only considered hyperactive because I like to stay busy and see things done and completed while moving to the next project or need. But I have found out that most of the world is not like that, and usually doesn't care for hyperactive people. It seems everyone wants to slow us go-getters down.

As I mentioned, as a young adult working and pastoring my first church I came across Isaiah 40:31 and it spoke strongly to me. No, God was not telling me to stop or even to slow down, but set a pace that did not get ahead of what He wanted to teach me and to a pace that others could travel at also. Then as I began to claim this verse and apply it to my life I found so much truth in it. I discovered you can fly as an Eagle when you're not just working for the Lord but working with Him and His Church. I hope you see what I'm trying to say. Alone, it is difficult to even get off the ground, almost impossible, but with the help of others who He has called, and as He strengthens us, all things are possible. Eagles do not find it hard to fly, because they don't depend on themselves as much as they trust in the wind, for without the wind beneath their wings they would not fly.

This concept of flying like an Eagle does not only apply toward projects around the church and the commission the church has to reach others. It also applies to our daily walk. The average American is not hyperactive but hyper-selfish. We see it, we want it, we get it, without considering the real cost. Not realizing that debt is a bondage that may allow us to have what we think we desire, while keeping us from having that which we really need. Getting that which we desire is what destroys homes. The house may be beautiful but the home does not exist because there is no time for one another, and without the unified support that God designed for us to have in a home, the home cannot fly, neither can you.

Do you find yourself tired, not able to rest? Is it because, though you are part of a busy world, but in reality you are alone? Are you working for things you desire, thinking they will satisfy your lust and bring you happiness? How long has it been since you soared like an Eagle and truly enjoyed the pleasures that God gave us freely? No, you may not need to stop dead in your tracks, but you may need to reevaluate your priorities and begin to move at a pace in your life, to which the One, who will help you soar, is at. "But they that wait upon the LORD shall renew *their* strength; they shall mount up with wings as eagles; they shall run and not be weary, and they shall walk and not faint (Isaiah 40:31 KJV)"

We Remember

For the first time in my life that I can remember, I have had to evacuate. But it was not my home as many of our neighbors further west of us had to evacuate because of Gustav, the hurricane. The reason I had to evacuate is that we had set up camp at St. Andrews State Park, which is on the Bay of the Gulf at Panama City Beach. We had come in Sunday morning for church and were planning on returning Sunday evening after church, but I received a call after our morning worship service, informing me that because of Gustav and Hanna the Governor had ordered that all State Parks in Florida be evacuated by three pm. I didn't quite make the three pm deadline, but Thomas and I were able to pull out before four. We did it in such a hurry it took Judy and me most of Monday morning to get every-thing back like it should be. Though I was one of the last to pull out, I was not alone. When we were pulling out I spoke to some that were leaving as we were, and they were complaining that they thought that the evacuation was premature.

Though most of us probably would not have lost much in value if the storm had destroyed what we had at the campsite, considering we had had enough cense to get ourselves out had it got bad. But as I was rushing around and nothing was going just as it should, I thought of all those who had learned a very valuable lesson a few years ago with Katrina and Rita and now again were not leaving campsites but had left homes and memories to protect that which is most valuable, life and family.

As I think of these acts of nature as some call them and others refer to them as acts of God, I once again noticed that for the most part we are given warnings that we might prepare for the worst when God allows nature to act. But as this Thursday is September 11th, I am also reminded of a tragic anniversary of evil men hurting and destroying innocent life, with no warning at all, just evil being evil. We now remember this day as Patriots Day, not to remember the evil, but to remember why we as nation are involved in wars around this globe. Because when good men get comfortable, evil men will raise their ugly heads to destroy the peace, until the Prince of Peace rules from His throne (Isaiah 9:6).

Yes, natural disasters can often create and bring great tragedy to our lives. But the worst tragedies take place when that which is evil set out with the intent to destroy lives, by men, and give no warning. Innocent civilian lives were taken as war was declared on America seven years ago. This is the type of tragedy we need to continue to have in the media and in our hearts. By the way, I still wear Red every Friday to show my support for our troops who have answered the call to those who have declared war on us. As we have now designated September 11th as Patriots Day, a day to remember the day that so many lost their lives so tragically, and the many heroes who did all they could to help others, and those who have reached out to the many, many families that were effected that day. And everyday since then as our armed forces have stepped up to the line and are trying to bring justice in this situation. May we not forget to lift our soldiers up in our prayers as they protect this great nation, may we also remember to pray for our political process of electing leaders and for those elected, that God will guide their thoughts to ever be wise to protect us from evil. And may we not be ashamed to raise our flags and let Ol' Glory fly high across this wonderful land the Lord has so richly blessed.

Jeremiah speaks to us in Lamentations 3:19-23 as he says, "Remember my affliction and my bitterness, the wormwood and the gall! My soul continually thinks of it and is bowed down within me. But this I call to mind, and therefore I have hope: The steadfast love of the LORD never ceases, his mercies never come to an end; they are new every morning; great is thy faithfulness (KJV).

What a Difference a Day Makes

One of the things that Judy and I have really enjoyed since we moved to Florida ten years ago are evening or over night trips to the Gulf. One of the things I have discovered on our trips often back to the same place, is that the beach is never exactly the same as it was the last time we were there. Isn't that great? Most of you will say no, because for some reason most people that I have worked with in church don't like change. But if they would only study God and His Holy Word they would realize that though He never changes He likes and created change.

After my granddaddy Tyson received Christ as his Lord he truly changed, for before his conversion he was an alcoholic and bar room brawler. But what a wonderful change took place in his life when he met Christ. His favorite song became "Time Has Made a Change in Me." If each one of us would take an honest look at ourselves we would have to confess that great changes have occurred in our life, some good, and some bad. Our bodies change to being larger or smaller, with less hair and more flexible skin, but hopefully we get wiser, which I think is what God intended to take place. God knew that we needed change in our lives even though we fight change. Most of us fight change because when we began to allow the change that God wants to bring in our lives; we become more of what He wants us to be, rather than what we had in mind. But just like the beach, if you know someone who has truly let God change their attitude, their desires and even their habits to be that which He wanted them to be, you will find they have found peace and joy, in being all that God intended for them to be.

God is a God of change, and He can cause these dramatic changes to take place in only a day. Think about it. There was a day when the entire universe was nothing but blackness and emptiness, in just a day He filled it with light and life. There was a time when all mankind longed for a Savior to come, and in the matter of a day, he sent His only Son and what a difference He made in this world, a difference that no one can deny, as our calendars count from His date of birth. The world thought they could destroy Him, but what a difference He made in just one day as He defied death, Hell and the grave, and rose victoriously. One of the greatest differences that I have seen in my life is how He has changed me and it all began the day I accepted His simple promise that He died that I might live, that He rose victoriously that I might have victory, and that He ascended to Heaven that I would be able to continue to live within His power filled with the Holy Spirit.

Everyday He continues to change the world and lives, one by one and day by day. Have you allowed

Him to be Lord and Master of your life? I hope so, because soon there is going to be a day, which the world will remember more so than it does the day that Christ came to earth, even more than the day He died and even the day He rose victoriously. It's the day He returns for His bride, the born-again church. That day there will be great changes take place in the local church and the world.

As I think about the beach and the changes that take place daily, and that Sunday the world will celebrate that He rose from the grave, I get excited because I am also aware of the changes that He has made in me and for this reason I look forward to every new day, just to see what new changes He will again bring in me. Praise the Lord Christ lives today, He is not in the grave but on The Throne, His Throne. We have so much to celebrate because as the angel said in Matthew 28: 5 -6 "Do not be afraid, for I know that you seek Jesus who was crucified. He is not here; for He is risen, . . ." (NKJV).

Hermit Crab

Every time we get to go to the beach, whether with grandchildren or just Judy and I, there is one creature that for some reason or another seems to always get someone's attention, the Hermit crab. I've noticed that the ones at St. Andrew State Park usually have fairly small shells, but the children seem to always to be amazed by them, especially at how fast they can craw up in their shell, and at how hard, and almost impossible it is to get them out of their beautiful shells that people want to take home. I've also noticed the crabs and the shells are just a little larger just across the channel at Shell Island, and on up in the bay at Bay Point they are quite a bit larger. But no matter where you may find them, you will notice that every Hermit crab seems very attached to its shell.

First of all I am not a shell or Hermit crab expert. And I hope I am right about what I understand about the Hermit Crab. It seems to make sense, because unlike the turtle or other creatures with shells, the Hermit crab is not attached physically to his shell, though he carries it at times as though he is. It is my understanding that the Hermit Crab takes his shell from another creature, and as he gets larger himself, he looks for a larger shell. But in retrospect the shell is not truly his, but you sure wouldn't know it by looking at them together.

A few weeks ago while watching some of these larger Hermit Crabs move around Bay Point, I thought about these things, that I think that I know about them, and began to look around at the things that we people occupy and get so attached to. The way that we get attached to cars, houses, boats and things in general, you would think we were born with these things attached to us. While in reality if the banks or finance companies hadn't held them for collateral, which means they actually own them, we wouldn't have them. But on top of all that, there is nothing that we have that did not come from that which God created, and since He created all from nothing, it all actually belongs to Him. So it seems that we are nothing more than some very large Hermit Crabs, swapping about trying to see who can get the largest shell to claim as ours, a shell that someone else will soon claim for theirs as soon as we drop it.

There is one particular shell, like the turtle that we also get very attached to and that is this wonderfully designed body the Lord created for us to enjoy while we are here on this earth as pilgrims. But one day we will also drop this shell, and for those who have chosen to serve our Lord Jesus Christ for eternity, we will then begin to enjoy our eternal home (shell) with Him. Now that's exciting, if you ask me!

"For we know that if our earthly house, *this* tent (shell), is destroyed, we have a building from God, a house not made with hands, eternal in the heavens.

For in this we groan, earnestly desiring to be clothed with our habitation which is from heaven, if indeed, having been clothed, we shall not be found naked. For we who are in *this* tent (shell) groan, being burdened, not because we want to be unclothed, but further clothed, that mortality may be swallowed up by life. Now He who has prepared us for this very thing *is* God, who also has given us the Spirit as a guarantee. So *we are* always confident, knowing that while we are at home in the body (shell) we are absent from the Lord. For we walk by faith, not by sight. We are confident, yes, well pleased rather to be absent from the body and to be present with the Lord" (2 Corinthians 5:1 - 8 NKJV with "shell" added). I personally hope you have received the guarantee, because that is the only shell that will last forever.

Hot Coals

Last Friday Judy and I were able to take a quick camping trip and spend some time with one of our grandsons, Brandon. Brandon is eight and as most eight year olds, very observant and smart, and knows it. I had a special opportunity to see him experience life and actually comprehend and learn something without it coming from a book.

After he joined us at the camp site, Judy remembered we had some marshmallows in the camper, and wanted a camp fire. So Brandon watched and helped as I built the fire. After roasting, or actually burning the marshmallows and having our fill, which does not take long, Brandon's interest returned to the fire. After a while he realized I was letting it die down. So he started looking for ways in which to keep the fire burning. He soon discovered small sticks from trees and rocks lying around the camp area and ask if he could throw them in the fire, and later discovered leaves, pine needles and pine cones and again asked if he could add them to the fire. So with permission and with caution he began to add these items to the fire and soon learned: rocks don't burn, sticks burn good, pine needles make a pretty display as they burn quickly, but leaves and especially pine cones make a large fire, for a little while. But the greatest lesson came as the source of his adding to the fire was no longer available and only red-hot coals were left.

At that point I began to share with him and let him illustrate how to keep those coals hot. He soon discovered, keep the coals close and they will stay hot, but spread them apart and they begin to get cold and die. Which I'm sure many of you already knew, and probably know where I'm going with these natural illustrations. For there are times we meet people who are burning hot for the Lord and all of a sudden, you couldn't get a witness for the Lord out of them if you held a gun to them. Like leaves, pine cones and pine needles they looked good for a while, but there never was anything solid about them. Their fire was all visual while there was no deep commitment and dedication that comes from having a strong daily walk with the Lord through His Word.

Then there are those who shine for our Lord for many years, then all of a sudden their glow for the Lord is gone, and their priorities in life have changed. But it is easy to spot what the problem is as you notice they have moved away from the center. They no longer are gathering with the family of God around the Lords table (the church) where we as Disciples of Christ are fed, challenged and encouraged. From the hot and cold coals we can definitely understand why the Lord had the writer of Hebrews write, "not forsaking the assembling of ourselves together, as is the manner of some, but exhorting one another, and so much the more, as you see the Day approaching" (Hebrews 10:25 NKJV). You and I need our local church so that we can stay hot for our Lord in representing Him in the cold, cruel world, for if we pull apart our glow (witness) for Him is dim and ineffective.

The Purposeful Pelican

A few weeks ago Judy and I went fishing with friends; we began our fishing trip that day at the Jetties at St. Andrew State Park. Because of the wind we soon moved to the pier, because no one was catching anything we then moved to the boat dock. You can easily tell it does not take much for me to get bored when fishing.

Since I am usually the first one to leave the truck and to get to the place we are going because I walk fast (If you haven't figured it out yet, I'm hyperactive), I had the opportunity to witness something the others with me did not see. As I was about half way down the dock, there it was, in front of me, on the dock, in the path that I would be going, a Pelican. So I slowed my walk down as I approached the big bird, with long legs, an even longer neck and a beak as long as a baseball bat. Actually there were several other Pelicans all around me, but not on the dock. Though they were all doing about the same thing, this particular one really got my attention, basically because of where he was, as he was doing what Pelicans do best, looking for food. As I got closer to this beautiful creation of God, standing on the same dock with me, which because of his height he could almost look me in the eyes. He definitely knew I was close by but did not seem concerned as he had his attention on a young man and his approximately ten year old son, which were right in front of him. So close if he stretched out his neck he could have touched them. As I watched what he was doing and he watched what they were doing I spoke with the man and boy who was fishing for bait fish. The young dad said that the Pelican had been standing in that same place watching them put their catch in the cooler for a very long time. Of course we all know what the Pelican was doing, he was looking for somebody to drop their catch or preferably leave the cooler open, so he could get his next meal, easily.

Soon another person came toward the Pelican from the other direction so the Pelican took flight. I then proceeded to my destination at the end of the dock to do a little fishing, little being the definitive word. It did not take me long to get bored fishing off the dock. I then began to think like the Pelican, there has to be an easier way; I think they call it the Fish Market at Winn-Dixie. So on my way back to land, from the dock, there they were again, Pelicans just standing around. While I was fishing I did witness a couple of them make a beautiful flight with the help of their large wing span and then drop swiftly from the air, inserting that baseball bat length beak into the waters beneath, retrieving dinner, then swiftly floating back up to the blue sky above. Watching them retrieve their next meal so effortlessly and beautifully proved that it was not that difficult for the Pelican to get his next meal. So as I walked by these large unusual birds with their long beak's standing unconcerned about their surroundings, I asked the Pelican that was closest to me at the time a question. Because as I was admiring his stately stand, I first heard myself saying, "Thank you Lord that you did not give me a beak and neck that long", I then said out loud, "Mr. Pelican, what is your purpose in life?" To which I soon heard one of the young people who were with us, whom I did not realize was standing that close by say, "Oh no, our pastor is witnessing to a Pelican."

The beautiful thing about all of nature is that all creation seems content with their purpose in life, except mankind. God created man with a body and mind that seems so superior to all the others, yet we fail to be content with our purpose. Many continue from day to day searching to fill that vacuum in their soul that only a relationship with God can fill. As God created man in His image for a greater purpose declaring, "For I know the thoughts that I think toward you, says the LORD, thoughts of peace and not of evil, to give you a future and a hope" (Jeremiah 29:11 NKJV). Though man tries to fill that vacuum with things that are immoral and un-natural, they will not find peace until they trust Him and find His will for their life, thus discovering their true purpose. "For by Him all things were created that are in heaven and that are on earth, visible and invisible, whether thrones or dominions or principalities or powers. All things were created through Him and for Him" (Colossians 1:16 (NKJV).

The One That Got Away

We had a very interesting Memorial Day weekend, as we had a great service Sunday at the church and honored those who had given their all that we might enjoy the great freedom we enjoy here in America. The Lord led me to preach on the subject "Freedom Worth Dying For" using the scripture of John 8:31-36 where Jesus told those listening, which were mostly descendants of Abraham, ""If you abide in My word, you are My disciples indeed. And you shall know the truth, and the truth shall make you free." They answered Him, "We are Abraham's descendants, and have never been in bondage to anyone. How can You say, 'You will be made free'?"" Sounds like most Americans I know, but "Jesus answered them, "Most assuredly, I say to you, **whoever commits sin is a slave of sin**. And a slave does not abide in the house forever, but a son abides forever. Therefore if the Son makes you free, you shall be free indeed.""(NKJV) In this text we found that though you may look free as people look at you from the outside, most are not free inside because we see the results of sin everyday on the news, most people are a slave to sin (adultery, fornication, homosexuality, alcohol, drugs, tobacco, debt, lust, hate, greed, gossip, PRIDE, etc.).

And a lesson that came up during the message that I think will be remembered the most is "your freedom ends, where mine begins", or vice versa. In other words, when the traffic light turns green for you, my freedom ended because it turned red on my side, this is a lesson that can be applied to most of our lives. But true freedom only comes when we are willing to die to ourselves so that we can come alive in Christ, thus choosing the best slavery, because everyone is a slave to something or someone. I have chosen and you can choose to allow Christ and His Word to be that which you are enslaved, because He paid the ultimate price upon the cross that we might be set free from the bondage that sin places each of us.

On Monday I also witnessed the scriptures come alive and be fulfilled right before my eyes. Friends had invited us to go with them down to the jetties and go fishing. Actually seven of us packed up and took off down to the Gulf that morning. The wind was a little too rough for us to fish from the jetties so we later went over to the dock and began to fish. A lot of other people had the same idea, but nobody was catching anything but a few small sharks, which they where throwing back. When it seemed that everyone was just getting good practice at casting, it happened. I thought my hook was hung on something, but I kept trying to bring it in as I had when it had gotten hung on the rocks at the jetties. I never broke my line, because with a little patience and persistence I had always been able to get it undone before, so I kept on trying this time. Sure enough, as the end of my line got closer to the dock and began to come to the top, I noticed it was still hard to pull in. As I looked over the dock to see what the problem was, I saw it, the prettiest twelve to fourteen inch Flounder that had been caught that morning from the dock. I know it was, because it was the only one caught that morning. Actually none us are much of what you would call fishermen, because we didn't even take anything to put our catch in. I happened to have a plastic sack that they had given me at the store when I purchased some frozen shrimp for bait. So the smart guy that I am, I put my Flounder in the bag and began walking back to the truck to put him on ice. BUT!!, on the way I saw some strangers looking over the side of the dock at the fish swimming by that no one was catching, and I just had to show them my catch. As I opened the bag so they could see it, they were so interested I just had to open it a little more, THEN ALL OF A SUDDEN the Flounder, jumped out of my hand, went over the dock rail and all the way back into the water. When I went fishing that morning I was not a fisherman, but when I left I was, because I now have the story of the big one that got away. For an hour or so, the people that I had showed the fish to when it jumped over the rail, stayed there on the dock and told everyone that walked by about the one that got away and pointed me out. Oh by the way, I never caught anything else that day, but just before we headed home, Judy, my wife, caught a twenty-four inch trout, and she didn't let it get away, plus she has pictures. With that in mind, you now know the rest of the story.

The moral of the story is, The Word of God, The Bible, is true and alive, not in part but in the whole, never doubt it. "Pride goes before destruction, And a haughty spirit before a fall" (Proverbs 16:18 NKJV).

Follow The Leader

This past Christmas, Judy gave me a Garman, that's one of those satellite navigation devices. She thought it might help us get where we intend to go, seeing as so often when traveling we get lost and have to stop and ask directions. When we travel I always like to have a map, but you can't drive and look at a map at the same time. So most the time, I'm the pilot (driver) and she's the navigator. She's gotten pretty good after thirty-one years of training (lol). I hope everyone knows what "lol" means, it's one of those internet terms, and means "laugh out loud". But she is also a person that likes gadgets and technology, so she bought the Garman for me, again "lol".

To get to the point, I've used it a few times now and we've used it a few times together, but I have not really learned to trust it, in that a few times it led me to the wrong place. Judy tells me that equipment like this is only as good as the operator (ouch). But this past Thursday, Friday and Saturday we were traveling to Fort Gaines, Georgia to go camping with friends. We had a great time and a great fish fry on the lake, along with two wonderful breakfasts. But the interesting part of the trip was getting there, and we vowed not to tell, and we didn't while we were camping, but now I will tell you.

First of all, we thought we knew how to get where we were going. We had been by the camp ground, Cotton Hill, at least once, if not twice. Plus we had written instructions that Barbara e-mailed me, plus she had told me how to get there. But! We had decided to turn the Garman on, and see what it said. Judy was operating it this time. And as we were traveling north of Dothan on Highway 431, long before we got to where we were to turn right, it told us to turn left, off of a four lane divided highway onto a small two lane road. I knew something was wrong, and refused to make the turn. Oh, by the way, we are driving a thirty-six foot long, wide body diesel motor home. But it just kept on telling us we needed to turn left, but I refused. Further on down the road, Judy said she had gotten it corrected, basically saying, the operator problem was fixed (wink). But then it happened again, the Garman wanted us to turn right about ten miles earlier than our instructions said we should. So again I refused to turn, but again it kept on saying turn at every right turn, so I decided why not. It took us on some back roads through the country and through many, many turns. It even lead us through the middle of a pasture, yes it was paved, but barely wide enough for the wheels of the motor home. Eventually it did lead us back to the route, where we wanted to be. We admit it was a scenic trip, but not the road I would have chosen to drive a motor home on.

When we did get to Fort Gaines it wanted me to make a left turn on the first road that sort of makes a town square. I thought I remembered Barbara saying it would do that, but that we should take the next turn, which I did. Then again the Garman tried to get me back on the right path, but this time we went on another very narrow, hilly road with trees hanging over the road so low that it looked as though it was a tunnel for small cars. But there was no other way to go, so we plugged through very carefully and guess what? When we got to the other side, there was our road we needed and would have been on if I had only listened to the Garman.

You probably already know where I'm going with this. Maybe you've been there before yourself. We have the best roadmap of all for life in the Bible and the leading of the Holy Spirit. But why do we so often question Him, Who made us or ignore Him, when He not only knows us best, but He knows what is best for us. He is also like the Garman, but in a better way, even if we have chosen to take the wrong turn in life, and have gotten in a situation that seems impossible to get out of. If we will be obedient, it may get more difficult before it gets better, and it may hurt our pride and many other things, but He will lead us to the place designed for us, even before we where conceived. And there we will find His joy and peace and a place where we can rest in Him, our Lord and Savior Jesus Christ. Acts 2:28 says, "You have made known to me the ways of life; You will make me full of joy in Your presence" (NJKV).

Ants

S ome of the reasons Judy and I enjoy camping so much is that every time we go we meet some of the nicest people, make new friends and have an adventure that we will never forget (Some we will talk about and some we won't). We never plan the adventure, it just happens, but we enjoy the fact that we can look back on a trip and always discover that we have something to laugh about.

Our latest RV trip was Labor Day weekend. We set up camp on the East Bank of Lake Seminole just out from Chattahoochee. Friday and Saturday were very pleasant days, the weather was perfect. We met some old friends and made some new ones, and were even able sit and watch a few alligators float by.

But several weeks before we made this trip, which was our first trip to this camp ground, I was warned by a couple who had been there before and was going to be there that Monday about the ants. They said to be sure to spray for the ants.

If I must admit it, I forgot what they had said, until we got there. When checking in, the host family reminded me what they had said and again warned us about the ants. Even told us what to purchase and how to spray for them. So spray we did, three different times on Friday just to be sure.

As I have mentioned, Friday and Saturday were wonderful, Judy and I were able to get some much needed rest. We came back in on Sunday morning for church and returned to the RV Sunday evening after church. But Monday was a very different day; the ants had found a way around the spray. They were on the inside and outside of our RV, they were everywhere! We sprayed again and again, and still there were ants.

As I watched what seemed like thousands of these little creatures proudly marching back and fourth, greeting each other, as they emptied our cabinets I was reminded of the wise words of Solomon. "Go to the ant, thou sluggard; consider her ways, and be wise" (Proverbs 6:6 KJV).

The first thought that came to my mind, as I considered what I was watching and what Solomon had said, was, how much more effective we as followers of Christ could be, if we were as considerate of others as the ants are of each other, so that we would stop and tell everyone we meet about the blessing of having a great relationship with our Lord Jesus Christ. Or if we would just stop and greet each other with a Holy kiss, as mentioned in 2 Corinthians 13:11-14, encouraging each other as we joyfully march through this life together.

As I continued thinking of how I wish we could teach this wonderful lesson of sharing the "Good News", I was abruptly reminded that there are many who do work like the ants by sharing everything they know (or think they know) but they do it so they can destroy and hurt other people. They spread gossip instead of the Good News of the Gospel. They talk about others instead of the blessings that God has given us.

The more I thought about it, the more I begin to think about the many good things that God had given us, such as a tongue, which we can use to share words of encouragement and love. Yet I thought, how sad it is that we allow that which God intended to be used to bless as a means of destruction and hurt.

The ants accomplish so much for the benefit of all, because they work together, encourage each other and do not worry who gets the credit. If only we could be as considerate as the ant.

Clear Rain

Have you ever thought about how wise and wonderful Jehovah God is? We have been told that He is omniscient, all knowing. But have you really thought about what that means? Especially when it comes to creation, how that He took nothing, absolutely nothing and made everything just right, just like it is. That's why the theory of evolution will always have huge holes in it. Because in the theory of evolution you can easily see that it is man's idea. Man decides to make something, such as an automobile, but from conception they have to continually change it, finding better ways to make it better. If man was so intelligent, why didn't they just start with the best, and stay with it like God did?

Have you ever thought to stop and Praise God because that rain is clear, that grass and trees are green, that the clouds are white on a blue canvas? Have you ever thought that we should be thankful that storm clouds are dark? That's right, I'm thankful that storm clouds are dark, they give me a warning that a storm is coming. That is so awesome if you think about it.

This really struck me the Friday before Labor Day, while driving our motor home toward the camp. It was then that I began to see the real beauty in the way that God created everything, and that He has never had to change it, because He did it right the first time.

We were driving East on I-10 headed for the East bank of Lake Seminole, just out from Chattahoochee. It began to rain; actually it was one of those "came on down" drenching rains. The motor home, like many large trucks and buses, has two separate wiper motors, but they are both controlled by the same switch. The wiper on the right side began to act up; it began to do all kinds of crazy things, even crossed over to the left side and got hung. So to save the motor, I turned the wipers off. But to my amazement it wasn't that bad! With the aerodynamics design of the windshield and the fact that rain is clear; it actually became an enjoyable ride. But that is when I began to be thankful that God had made rain and all water clear and not red, yellow, blue, orange or black.

Could you imagine what kind of a mess I would have been in if the rain was a dark red or black, and the wipers wouldn't work? Can you imagine the kind of mess it would make in our yards, on the roads and especially our clothes and skin? You remember the experiments in middle school where we put food coloring in the water and then stuck a celery stalk in it? You have to admit, water by any other color, just would not be appealing or refreshing. Neither would the trees and grass be as luscious if they were any other color, nor the sky for that matter.

If it happens to be raining where you are, be thankful the rain is clear. If it happens to be stormy, praise the Lord for the dark cloud that arrived first and will soon pass. If the Sun is shining bright and the grass is green, be comforted in the warmth and thankful that the grass is not hot-pink. If it happens to snow where you are, praise the Lord for the whiteness of the snow that lightens a dark winter's sky, and thankful that snow is not bright orange. Be thankful today that when God does something, He does it right the first time, from the creation of this earth to the redemption of man. 1 Thessalonians 5:16-18 says that we should "Rejoice evermore. Pray without ceasing. In every thing give thanks: for this is the will of God in Christ Jesus concerning you" (KJV). Most of all be thankful that God created you and has given us His Bible to tell us how precious you are to Him and that someone in your life has shared His love with you. Because the truth of the matter is, He made rain clear, grass green and the sky blue, because He knew it would be most pleasing to you. May we live our life being pleasing to Him!

In the Sonlight

Judy and I enjoy walking the beach in the evening. Many times as we would walk or even ride along the Gulf, I have noticed how the sun reflection on the water seemed to follow us wherever we went until it set. We were enjoying one those walks last week as the sun seem to be just feet from touching the water. As we walked Judy was looking down to find shells as I admired and wondered about all that was around us. The sun was a bright Orange, white clouds seemed to just want to be near the Sun, and because of their nearness they took on a lighter color Orange of that which the Sun was. The sky was a deep glowing blue that took your breath. The Sea was a still scary calm with aqua splendor about it that was glittering. Then across this beautiful aqua shimmering Sea, from the Sun to us came an Orange, almost Red path, which seemed to say, this is just for you. Again I noticed that this beautiful lighted path from the Sun to us seemed to follow us wherever we went until the Sun set so slowly touching the sea and then gradually disappearing as the earth became between it and us.

I began to praise the Lord and thank Him for letting me enjoy His beautiful creation. As I began to wish we had a camera to save this beautiful moment so that all could share this with us, I began also to think of the significance of this moment.

Think of how awesome it is that just as the clouds changed because of their relationship with the Sun, so should you and I change to be more like Christ as we draw near to the Son of God. But the most significant part of this walk came as that bright orangey red path followed our every move. Through this walk I realized that no matter where I went in this world, whether forward or backward, fast or slow, the Son still went with me. The only thing that would keep me from seeing and feeling His presence was when I let the world itself get between the Son and me. At that moment the light is darkened and I begin to fill empty and alone. But just as the Sun sets behind the world, the Sun is not gone forever nor that relationship destroyed. Lord willing, there will be the horizon of another beautiful day, in which that lighted path will return.

Though I may let wants, desires, habits, addictions and selfishness of this world come between the Son and me, and though my days may get dark and become empty and scary, it does not mean He has forsaken me, nor have I destroyed our relationship. He has only let me endure the night without Him that I might be eager to repent and experience the Sonlight of the morning.

Morning Star

Judy and I enjoy walking the beach in the evening. Many times as we would walk or even ride along the Gulf, I have noticed how the sun reflection on the water seemed to follow us wherever we went until it set. We were enjoying one of those walks as the sun seems to be just feet from touching the water. As we walked Judy was looking down to find shells, as I admired and wondered about all that was around us. The sun was a bright orange, white clouds seemed to just want to be near the Sun, and because of their nearness they took on a lighter color orange of that which the Sun was. The sky was a deep glowing blue that took your breath. The Sea was a still scary calm with aqua splendor about it that was glittery. Then across this beautiful aqua shimmering Sea, from the Sun to us came an orange, almost red path, which seemed to say, this is just for you. Again I noticed that this beautiful lighted path from the Sun to us seemed to follow us wherever we went until the Sun set so slowly touching the sea and then gradually disappearing as the earth became between it and us.

I began to praise the Lord and thank Him for letting me enjoy His beautiful creation. As I began to wish we had a camera to save this beautiful moment so that all could share this with us, I began also to think of the significance of this moment.

Think of how awesome it is that just as the clouds changed because of their relationship with the Sun, so should you and I change to be more like Christ as we draw near to the Son of God. But the most significant part of this walk came as that bright orangey red path followed our every move. Through this walk I realized that no matter where I went in this world, whether forward or backward, fast or slow, the Son still went with me. The only thing that would keep me from seeing and feeling His presence was when I let the world itself get between the Son and me. At that moment the light is darkened and I begin to feel empty and alone. But just as the Sun sets behind the world, the Sun is not gone forever nor that relationship destroyed. Lord willing, there will be the horizon of another beautiful day, in which that lighted path will return. Though I may let wants, desires, habits, addictions and selfishness of this world come between the Son and me, and though my days may get dark and become empty and scary, it does not mean He has forsaken me, nor have I destroyed our relationship. He has only let me endure the night without Him that I might be eager to repent and experience the Son-light of the morning.

This also drew my thoughts toward the return of Christ for His church. Many have come to ignore that Christ has promised that He will soon return for those who are looking for Him, because it has been over two-thousand years, and the world seems to continually get darker (evil and immorality spreading so fast from every corner and aspect of this world). Many are denying and forgetting Christ said "Surely I come quickly" three times in the last chapter of the last book which the Lord gave to us. That "Surely I come quickly" lets us know that it is eminent; it is like a shadow that has been hanging over mankind all the time. It means it could happen anytime, and when He does return, there is a series of events that nothing can change that will occur. And one of the reason I believe His return is right upon us, is because in that last chapter of that last book which is "The Revelation of Jesus Christ" Christ refers to Himself as "bright and morning star, (Revelation 22:16 KJV). The "morning star" is the star that shines just at the end of the darkness and at the beginning of the dawn. It is the brightest star in the sky. When things are about as dark as they possibly can get, then the bright and morning star begins to shine. Our world seems to have turned its back on its Creator and Lord; it seems as though we are at the darkest point that we could possibly be. Just as I believe the sun will rise in the morning, I believe I will soon see "The bright and morning star" Christ Himself. I hope you are allowing Him to change you, as you draw close to Him, and because of your relationship with Him you are also eagerly waiting His return and sharing it with others.

Reflect His Image

Our home and church sits on a small hill over looking Blue Lake. Blue Lake is not that big of a lake, actually locals like to call it Blue Pond. Whatever you want to call it, it is a beautiful place, especially looking down from the church. From this view you look over the cemetery and through an oak tree with moss hanging low from it and three large wood crosses.

One evening as the sun had begun to set, I walked down toward the lake and I noticed such a wonderful calmness upon it. It was so calm that the pink clouds in the sky were also in the lake. It was hard to tell one from the other, it was such a beautiful reflection. It illustrated to me the joy of allowing the love and peace of Christ to reflect though us, in the calmness of our spirit. Then the next day or so I looked down toward the lake from the church and there was a breeze blowing. Because of the breeze the lake was very choppy, but the sun was shining and so the lake looked as though it was covered with large sparkling diamonds, what a sight it was. And again the Lord seemed to speak and say, when we allow Him to be reflected through our life in our calmness, when troublesome times do come, He will shine upon us and the world can still see His reflection in us. Then came Sunday, I looked down upon the lake again and saw a mixture of the two days. Parts of the lake where calm and reflecting the beautiful sunshine while there were spots that were choppy yet sparkling. That reminded me of my own life so often. Though it seems most of the time there is a concern or disturbance taking place, and it seems that God is using that to help me grow in my walk and even prepare me and others for something more, yet at the same time because of my trust in Him and His blessings, those chopping times seem to sparkle, while at the same time there are those beautiful calm spots that allow me to reflect upon His presence in my life.

Though I know I fail often, it is my prayer that, as I read His Word and spend time allowing Him to speak to me through His word and prayer, that others will see Christ in me and that He will be glorified. Paul spoke of that being transformed to His image in 2 Corinthians 3:18, but as He mentions, it can only happen as we seek His face and allow Him to own our life, face and attitude.

"But we all, with open face beholding as in a glass the glory of the Lord, are changed into the same image from glory to glory, even as by the Spirit of the Lord" (2 Corinthians 3:18 KJV).

Rain And Birds

Here in Florida we have a saying, "If you don't like the weather, wait fifteen minutes and it will change." The proof in the pudding was this morning. As I began getting ready for the day ahead I heard birds singing outside and they sounded so pretty as I began think, "Now this is going to be a beautiful day." But then I took notice that I heard something else, it was rain running off our metal roof. Then I thought of how God sends us showers of blessings. Then things changed again, the rains began to pour down as the wind blew and the thunder roared. Again I remind you that all this happened in less than 30 minutes. At this point I had not actually been out or even looked outside, but began to focus on what God had allowed me to hear, the sweet song of the birds, the refreshing sound of the falling rain, and then the alarming woosh of wind and rain. Have you ever noticed that you cannot have one of these with the other? While the wind is blowing hard and the rain is falling rapidly, you don't seem to notice that which comes with just a refreshing rain. And even when the rain is falling and adding its life-giving strength to the earth, you don't hear the birds sing. Oh yes, there was one more sound about an hour later, as the rain began to slow and the sky began to clear, tree frogs began to sound out their song of thanks for the rain.

As I began to praise the Lord for the opportunity of experiencing what I had experienced with just my ears, several scriptures came to mind and an old cliché. First there was Ecclesiastes 3:1 which says, "To everything *there is* a season, A time for every purpose under heaven:" Then a few verses down is Ecclesiastes 3:11-13 Solomon wrote, "He has made everything beautiful in its time. .....—it *is* the gift of God" (NKJV). In these verses Solomon is reminding us that life is a precious gift from God and that we should never take any part of it for granted, but enjoy every breath, even the storms have their purpose. This leads us to the old cliché, one that seems easier to smile about than actually follow through, "When life gives you lemons, make lemonade." This always makes me think of the instructive words of James 1:2, "My brethren, count it all joy when you fall into various trials..." Like the lemonade, his words seem to be difficult to digest at times. But as you read your Bible you will find many testimonies of people who followed the instructions of James chapter one and turned defeat into victory, and trials into triumph. Instead of being victims, they became victors. They experienced victories because they had walked with the Lord through storms before and could look back and count the blessings of how He did not remove the storm but walked with them through each and when the greater storms came their faith was secure in Him. I actually envision them as starting each morning with "Good morning Lord" and ending their day in His restful arms because they are assured that their faith, hope and life lay safely in His loving arms.

I'm not actually saying every cloud has a silver lining, but I am saying as we experience life, we must realize God has a purpose in all things, and that purpose is to bring us to know Him and experience His will for our life. It's like looking at the backside of a tapestry, a woven rug or needlepoint. From the backside most are ugly with loose ends dangling and colors that do not make sense. But please don't judge the worker or the work by looking at the wrong side, for when you turn it over you will see the beauty in the work. In the same way we are looking at the wrong side of life. Only the Lord sees the finished pattern. Let's don't judge Him or His work from what we see today, for if you're reading this, His work in you are not finished yet.

Another Cliché I like is "Outlook determines Outcome, and attitude determines Action." So no matter what this day offers you, please remember life is not an end within its self, it's only a wonderful time to prepare for the ultimate, Eternity (John 3:16; Romans 6:23; 10:9-13).

What You Don't See

While traveling east on Interstate 10, I happened to take notice as we crossed the Chipola River, that if it were not for the road sign telling us that we were crossing a river and that the bridge disrupted our smooth ride, we would probably not have taken any notice of it at all. Which is sad, for the Chipola River is a beautiful river. I know this because I canoed down it with Judy, my wife, our youngest son, Bryan, and friends.

I've been down many rivers in canoes, rafts and even tubes and whether it was calm water or swift water, it has always been time well spent. For it has been time spent sharing these adventures with family and friends, enjoying the beautiful scenery that the Lord has created all around us. When canoeing down the Chipola there are some of the most beautiful Cyprus trees growing in the midst of the clearest, deepest and calmest waters. From this Judy was able to take some wonderful pictures, which she has framed and shared with others. Actually you can view some of them on the Internet at "http://community.webshots.com/album/76679504QFHYqW" and Nadine Hall, a lady that works with her has taken these pictures and made a beautiful large painting that hangs in her office.

But as people travel Interstate 10 and cross the Chipola River at 70 plus miles per hour most give very little thought to the treasure they have just crossed, because from the Interstate with other things on your mind, all that you might notice is undergrowth around some still water, and a bump or two in the road as you cross the bridge. As I thought about the beauty of this river and the treasures that it hides, I thought about how the world views the Christian life. Individuals who do not have a relationship with Christ often cross a bump or two in their life as they speed by and they may take a glimpse off to the side and see what they refer to as religion. From where they are traveling it looks nostalgic and cluttered with a lot of undergrowth that has developed through the years, but nothing appealing enough to actually them slow down on their journey. A journey that has no apparent end in sight, but what they don't see is the disaster at the end of their journey. I would not mislead anyone and say the Christian life is slow and easy going like the Chipola. But when you walk hand and hand with my Lord Jesus Christ, there is a peace and serenity that you experience. And there is joy in the journey because you know that the beauty that you now enjoy, even in the midst of turmoil and trial, is just a foretaste of greater beauty at the end of this journey. Walking with Christ and knowing Him as your Lord and Savior is more than religion. It is a beautiful relationship that you cannot see or understand by a glimpse now and then as things interrupt your journey and you decide to look off for just a moment.

James chapter one talks about the joy that one can have in the midst of trials and even temptations as one looks to the Lord for wisdom. The next time your life is interrupted by something that causes you to question the journey that you are now traveling, take just a moment and pull off and take a closer look, and listen. You may be receiving an invitation from the Lord to change the direction that you are now going. It's an invitation, if you accept it, you will never regret receiving. There may still be some rough and deep waters, but they will be clear and refreshing as you travel with Him. That is a promise that I have experienced and you can too.(Luke 13:3; 1 Corinthians 15:3-4; Romans 10:9-13).

Impossible

Not only has this been a very hot summer, but for many it has been a very difficult summer. All of us from time to time experience disappointments, hurt and even repercussions from bad decisions. Often times as we look at life, it seems as though we have found ourselves between a rock and a hard place such as the Children of Israel did as they stood on the banks of the Red Sea, and Pharaoh's army was heavy on their trail. They had just escaped forty years of slavery and now it seemed as though they would either die in the wilderness, or return to Egypt as tortured slaves. Their future did not look very great at that point. But Exodus 14:29 tells us, "By faith (the Children of Israel) passed through the Red Sea as by dry land which the Egyptians trying to do the same thing were swallowed up by the water" (KJV).

Do you ever get in what seems to be impossible situations? Those times when you look behind you and you get distressed, and then you look out before you and you get depressed. What I'm asking is, do you have any rivers you think are un-crossable or any mountains you can't go over or tunnel through? Well, if you said yes, I have good news for you. For my Lord specializes in things thought to be impossible. If you are between a rock and a hard place, if you are in what seems to be an impossible situation, you've looked behind you and the army of discouragement and bondage are vastly closing in on you, and the Red Sea before you seems un-crossable, look to the Lord as Moses did. And then by faith, when He leads you forward, move forward and see what faith can do. Then find you a good Bible teaching and believing local church, where you can meet with other brothers and sisters in Christ who will pray with and for you as you pray with and for them, not some of this TV hyped-up stuff.

There's something that we often fail to take into consideration when we consider the Children of Israel and their crossing of the Red Sea. The children of Israel didn't have a whole lot of faith to begin with. Moses was the one who had the faith. In fact, they blessed Moses out on many occasions and said, "Man, why did you bring us out here, to drown?" (Exodus 10:14). They always cried and grumbled when they got in a hard spot, saying dumb things like, "it would be better for them to serve the Egyptians than to die in this wilderness" So what we need to see is how the faith of one man can lift the level of faith of others. We learn as children that fear is contagious, but faith is contagious as well. One person's fear can fill a whole crowd with fear, or one person's faith can fill a whole crowd with faith. Moses said to the people when they began to fear, "Fear not, stand still and see the salvation of the Lord. . . . For the Lord shall fight for you and you will hold your peace" (Exodus 14:11-14 KJV).

You know what happened next, don't you? When they started moving forward by faith, God took that Red Sea and simply parted the waters and then He put His vacuum cleaners there and sucked up all the water out of the sand and it was dry as dust. They went walking through the Red Sea on dry ground. That's what faith does. Faith leads you through the waters of impossibility. Actually the parting of the waters of the Red Sea is a great picture of the death, burial and resurrection of the Lord Jesus Christ and it gives us a beautiful picture of how our faith in Christ can deliver us from the bondage of sin. Dr. Jerry Vines once gave a wonderful definition of what living faith really is. He said, "Living faith is faith that believes what God said (in his Word) and acts upon it, regardless of the circumstances and consequences." You see that is what the Children of Israel did as they marched forward as God opened up the Red Sea. They trusted what God said and then acted on it regardless of circumstances or consequences. If you know Christ as your Lord, trust His Word and act upon it.

But also notice, that as the children of Israel went through, the Egyptians saw what was taking place and basically said, "Let's try that too." We also know the rest of the story, the same waters that delivered Israel destroyed Pharaoh's Army. The truth we learn from that is, though you can encourage others in their faith and they can encourage you by their testimonies, you will not win heaven or victories in your life, through the faith of others. You, yourself, must have a relationship with Christ, because, salvation does not come from acquaintance, a religious experience or exercise, but from a personal relationship with Christ as your Lord.

A Father's Influence

One of the most exciting things that I have had the privilege of doing as an adult was to go back to the city where I spent my childhood. We had first moved to Chicago Illinois when I was two. We moved back to the North Georgia Mountains while I was in Junior High, that's what we called Middle school back then. I had not had the privilege of going back to Chicago until 30 years later. In 1997 friends and family made it possible for me to attend the Write-To-Publish Conference at Wheaton College in Wheaton, Illinois, which is a suburb of Chicago. It was a very busy week as 140 writers and authors from five countries gathered to be enlightened and encouraged by the many editors and publishers that had gathered looking for new, fresh, and raw material (raw material, that's me).

The Conference, which was the purpose for the trip was very enlightening. Being there and having others who understand the burden that I have to share the things that God has given me beyond my local church was great. The reason for being there had actually begun about six years earlier as the Lord had placed a burden on my heart to write a few books. The first of which I have written, and that was why I was in Chicago, trying to learn how to get it published. As you guessed, it has yet to be published, but if I had never sat down to write it, I would not be writing to you today. As I look back I consider my trip to Chicago a success, mostly because it gave me an opportunity to look back at my past, as I never had done before.

As you can tell, while planning my trip to Wheaton College, I saw it as a great opportunity to check out the accuracy of my childhood memories. Since it had been such a long time since I had actually wandered the streets of that great city, that's what I did a lot of while we were there, wander the streets, mostly on my bike with my friend Steve.

On the flight back to Atlanta, my mind was not only spinning from all that I had absorbed at the conference, but also of my past. I realized that my past was made possible because of my parents. No, most of you would not have enjoyed living where we did, but it was the only life I knew, it was home.

I can now look back and see that the fifteen times that we moved before I turned twenty were not negative influences on my life, but positive. Living in a home where my dad basically moved us to Chicago from the Cotton Mill town of Trion Georgia to try to better his family, and feeling that the Lord was leading him in that direction, for it was there in Chicago the Lord called my dad to preach. It is there that dad helped establish a mission, and in that mission is where I received the Lord Jesus Christ as my Savior, just a few blocks from Wrigley field. No, our move to Chicago could not be considered all roses. Like all men who try to get out of a rut, dad seemed to get in situations that others would question, but I witnessed my dad always putting Christ first. Watching his life being lived out before me, allowed me to witness how the Lord takes care of those who put Him first as His word promises "But seek first the kingdom of God and His righteousness, and all these things shall be added to you" (Matthew 6:33 NKJV).

Today, I can truly say, I know that I would not be the person that I am today; if my dad had not risked everything, not only to better himself and his family, but to also follow Christ. You see, my testimony does not begin with my conversion, but with my conception and childhood. This is also true about you. Your parents had a great impact on the person you are today. Whether positive or negative, that influence is there. Even though some may look at me and say, "Oh that was a bad place to live as a child", but I can now say, "No, it was for my good", because all the moves, the people that I met and most of all our home was all a part of molding me into being the person that I am today.

This Sunday is Father's day. Don't forget to say, "thank you" to the man who shared his life with you, helping to mold you into the person you are today. Also, remember to worship and praise your heavenly Father who laid out the pattern that has formed you into the person you are and who you will be. Lastly, to all of you who are dads and are reading this today, please take notice of those around you, and know that every decision you make is influencing others in who they will become tomorrow. "Train up a child in the way he should go (live before them and be apart of their life), and when they are old they will not depart from it" (taken in part from Proverbs 22:6).

The Jesus Bomb

On The National Day of Prayer, (May 1, 2008) I gathered with a thousand other believers (as reported by Channel 7 news) around the lake in Defuniak Springs Florida. As we concluded our prayer time by praying for our soldiers serving in the military of this great land, singing "Amazing Grace" and "God Bless America" I looked around and saw a young lady walking through the park with a large cardboard sign hung over her body which read "Who Would Jesus Bomb?". I know that her intentions were to say that she did not support our soldiers or the war, and for some reason she was under the impression that neither would Jesus.

First of all I would say to her and to you, it is not her place, your place nor my place to say what Jesus would do today if He were here in bodily form. But praise the Lord I do have the scriptures, which tell me what He has done in the past and actually what He is doing today and what He will be doing in the future. And from what I read, it does not seem possible that this young lady has taken time to read her Bible before asking the question, because she would have discovered whom Jesus has bombed and who He could potentially choose to bomb.

If she had read the Bible she would have read where Jesus went into the Temple apparently twice (John 2:14-16 & Matthew 21:12-17) and threw the people and their stuff out who were abusing the purpose of the Temple and dishonoring the name of God, just as she was doing. To me that would be equivalent to bombing in His day. As she continued reading she would have read (Mathew 3:7; 12:34; 23:33) where Jesus called those in His day who claimed to speak for God in judging others "Viper, snakes and hypocrites". I would also call that a pretty large bomb that He threw at them that day.

Then if she believes as I do that Jesus Christ is God in His place in the Trinity, she would have also read that He destroyed Sodom and Gomorrah (Genesis 19) because He could not fine ten righteous men in them. The cities had become so infested by immorality that homosexuality had became the norm and was a mockery to God so much so that fire fell from the heavens and destroyed every living thing in them. That's what I would definitely call a Jesus Bomb. In reading the scripture she could also read in Joshua 6 & 7 where Achan had taken that which God had forbidden, Israel had lost the battle to Aia because of this one man's sin. In order for them to once again be victorious they had to deal with the sin in the camp, which they did by stoning and burning Achan and his family. I think this could also be called a Jesus Bomb. As you continue to read through the history of Israel in the Old Testament you will see time and time again where God raised up other nations to overtake them because "In those days there was no king in Israel; everyman did what was right in his own eyes" (Judges 17:6;21:25 NKJV), and because of this we see a lot more Jesus bombs.

With the previous information in mind, and the question before us, "Who Would Jesus Bomb?" do we know of a country or people group which sounds anything like those mentioned? The Barna Research Company released last week that in their research they have discovered that only 5% of Americans tithe to a church or charitable organization. That would tell me that there are less than 5% of Americans who are righteous as God was looking for in Sodom and Gomorrah. No, not because a person would tithe of the blessing that God has given them would make them a righteous person, but I believe it would be safe to say that a righteous person would tithe. As with Sodom and Gomorrah the immoral lifestyle of homosexuality seems to have infested this great nation. Plus where the Law of Moses condemns the murderer to death and protects children, today government and people want to protect and reward those who do crimes of murder by supporting them for life, and condemn innocent children to death through abortion. And on top of all that, Christians are not allowed to pray in public school or talk about the Bible in history or science class, but there are public schools that offer classes on the Koran, and if you are of the Islam faith you can leave class to go to pray. This attitude against Christianity has also carried over to the work place. The large department stores will not hire a person if they put on their application that they do not want to work on Sunday because it's the Lord's Day, but they will hire those of the Islam faith and allow them to have their religious days off and even give them opportunities to pray while on the clock.

As we look around us it looks as if there are more than one nation and people groups who are well over due a Jesus bomb. It also seems that this young lady and many more should not be condemning followers of Christ for praying for our soldiers, but should be thankful that they are also praying for her and this nation as a whole, as Moses did in Exodus 32 when God intended on dropping a very large Jesus bomb on them because they had created and were worshipping a golden calf. I personally believe the reason we have not experienced a Jesus bomb today is because there are those who are standing in the gap, pleading in the name of Jesus Christ for His mercy for others, as the message of repentance is being preached.

Y'all Pray For Me

B ack when our oldest son, Steven, was only three or four years old, Gatha, my wife's sister also had a son about the same age, Kevin. This would have been about thirty years ago, before churches such as ours had children's church. The children were expected to sit in church and behave. If they did not, they soon learned that there would be consequences to pay for their bad actions. Back then spanking a child was not considered child abuse. Matter of fact those who spared the rod (Proverbs 13:24) and did not bring their children to church and teach them to respect others and reverence the church were considered the child abusers (Proverbs 22:6).

The church we attended at that time, the Ridgecrest Baptist Church in Rossville Georgia, had several young couples, which meant there was usually a child or two, who from time to time would test the waters to see if the rules had changed since the last time they were in church. This particular Sunday, apparently Kevin had ignored the first two or three warnings that Gatha had given him. You know those warnings; first the stern look, if that didn't work then there was the shaking of the finger with the stern look, then finally, the last warning, the moving of the mouth with the stern look and the shaking of the finger which would say this is your last chance. After an understood third warning was ignored, then action had to be taken. It was then time to pay the consequences for ignoring the warnings, as the action began, everyone knew what was next. As Gatha picked Kelvin up in her arms and headed for the back boor, it happened to be one of those quiet times as the pastor was going up to the pulpit to begin his message. Kelvin definitely knew what was coming next. So in the quietness of the moment, his head perched above his mother's shoulders, Kevin cries out for everyone to hear "Y'ALL PRAY FOR ME!" To say the least, his cry for help changed the service, but it did not change the consequences he was due to pay.

As I began to think of that time again, I also realized that those actions of a child are so much like the action that adults also take in their lives and even a great nation follows those bad practices. We see the warnings, but we just continue to ignore them, I guess hoping that this time it will be different. But then we see the consequences approaching, and then we begin to cry out for help, but it's too late, the snow ball has already begun to roll and gather momentum.

Everyone seems concerned about our economy, and we should be. Many seem to be concerned about the direction this great country is headed, and again I think we should be. Companies are crying out to be bailed out, and most families' wish they also could be bailed out, all because we as individuals and as a nation have ignored the stern warnings from our Heavenly Father. We have bought things that we could not afford disregarding His warnings (Proverbs 2:7). This great nation that vowed to separate the State from the church, meaning that the government would not support a religion, many years ago adopted a godless religion, they called it Evolution and began to teach our children they came from tadpoles and monkeys. Basically saying to them they have no purpose, so with no purpose, the next generation began to murder its own offspring calling it convenience for the survivalist (Abortion). Because life had become basically insignificant, mankind began to ignore His creator and turned from the natural use of the human body, committing an abomination before God through Homosexuality. With all this, mankind has taught itself to disregard others to become only concerned about satisfying one's own desires. So we charge and get credit till there's nothing and no way to pay it back, so then we cry for a bail out, or we will just bankrupt, and start the process all over. Why? Because we see no reason why we should fix our problem, we just want a Band-Aid to make us feel better about what we have done. Because to fix the problem would mean that we would have to change the way we think and do things and that would hurt our feelings. It would also take too much time, work and sacrifice, which we are not accustomed to.

We tried government intervention many years ago because of bad management and called it the New

Deal and created Social Security, the government bailed the people out. Hopefully we have learned from the mistakes of our past, but I am afraid we have not. Because if we had, we would know that a Democracy does not fix its problems by turning to Socialism, we fix it by buckling down, becoming humble and obedient before our Heavenly Father, simply by returning to the God of our childhood, and the work ethics His taught and installed in us (2 Chronicles 7:14).

Love of God

If I've heard it once I've heard it a thousand times, "God loves everyone." But when that statement is made it normally makes me very uncomfortable because I normally have the feeling that I am in the presence of a person who has never read their Bible and who does not have a personal relationship with God through His Son Jesus Christ.

The first reason that I cringe when someone says "God loves everyone" is because normally they are defending an immoral act or attitude of someone and in doing so they are trying to justify their personal belief without truly taking what God has said into consideration. In doing so, they are adding to the scripture, which is God's word to His children, to which there is a warning. In The Revelation of Jesus Christ chapter 22 and verse 18 it says, "For I testify unto every man that heareth the words of the prophecy of this book, If any man shall add unto these things, God shall add unto him the plagues that are written in this book:" So my question is, "Where in the Bible does it say that God loves everyone?

It does say in 2 Corinthians 9:7 that God loves a cheerful giver. But I don't quite think that includes everyone, and besides that, Paul was addressing his statement to the church, not everyone. Also in 1 John 4:8 and 4:16 John states that "God is Love" which is actually a description of who He is, not what He does. John 3:16 helps us understand what it means to be loved by God in that it says, "For God so loved the world, that He gave his only begotten Son, that whosoever believeth in him should not perish, but have everlasting life" (KJV). In that verse did you see the key to God's love, in love God gave the most precious possession He had, His Son. But nowhere does it say He forced His love on anyone and everyone, His love must be received because it is a gift of Himself.

The truth that most people do not want to admit is that God was not made for man, but man was made for God. God made everything in the universe, but He desired a creation that would love Him because they desired and chose to love Him back, not because they where created to do so (much like a robot). So He allowed man to choose between Him and the pleasure of sin, immoralities for a season.

If one will read their Bible they will soon discover that yes "God is love" but that God also hates many things that people do. Malachi 2:16 says that God hates divorce. Isaiah 1:14 states that God hates appointed feasts which apply to holidays where people celebrate things of the earth and the universe. Psalm 11:5 tells us that God hates the wicked and people who love violence (Boy, does that cover a wide spectrum, especially as we look at what the most popular TV programs, songs and games of the day are). But I think the wise Solomon describes what God hates the best in Proverbs 6:16-

19 as he says, "These six things doth the Lord hate: Yes, seven are an abomination unto Him: A proud look, A lying tongue, Hands that shed innocent blood (Abortion), A heart that devises wicked plans (imaginations), Feet that are swift in running to evil, A false witness who speaks lies, and one who sows discord among brethren" (NKJV). Paul defines these abominations that God hates in more detail in Roman 1:18-32 where he lists the following: the worship of images of animals and the lust of human body, women lusting after women and men after men (Homosexuality), sexual immorality (Adultery, Fornication, and so forth), wickedness, covetousness, maliciousness, envy, murder, strife, deceit, whispers, back-biters, haters of God, violent, proud, boasters, inventors of evil things, disobedience to parents, undiscerning, untrustworthy, unloving, unforgiving and unmerciful. Woo! What a list. The sad thing that many forget, even today, is that through out history, because these things that God hates were left unchecked by the people, cities such as Sodom and Gomorrah, and nations such as the Great Rome Empire fell and where destroyed.

The real beauty of it all is the nature of God, that not only is He love, He is also a jealous and a Holy God. Because of His nature He can never allow those who commit these abominations into His presence, and because they, through their actions, reject His love He is forced by their decisions to cast them into outer darkness away from Him (Hell). But because of His nature of love for the world, and that He gave His Son that everyone could be forgiven <u>if they would repent</u> and turn from their wicked ways, He continues to send out the message of His love through His messengers of the church and tells us that we are to "Preach the word! Be ready in season *and* out of season. Convince, rebuke, exhort, with all longsuffering and teaching. For the time will come when they will not endure sound doctrine, but according to their own desires, *because* they have itching ears, they will heap up for themselves teachers; and they will turn *their* ears away from the truth, and be turned aside to fables" (2Timothy 4:2-4 KJV). And that is why I continue to take the stand that I do. Because God loved me and forgave me of my sins and gave me eternal life and because of His love which now dwells in me, I love you and desire that you also experience His love by receiving Him as your Lord and Savoir as you repent and turn from the things which are destroying you.

Ham and Eggs

We definitely are living in tragic times, when politicians are running their campaigns on a platform which promises to destroy the family by pledging their allegiance to those who are pushing this great nation to continue to murder innocent children through abortion and the immorality of the homosexual agenda. No wonder children are killing their parents, and plotting against their teachers and beating each other up so they can put a video on the internet. Parents have been killing children in America for more than thirty years in the name of convenience and calling it abortion. Children and adults have lost respect for themselves and for each other, which leads to the decay of the family, schools, churches, and our great country.

The real tragedy behind the tragic news is that we have forgotten the lesson our forefathers taught and fought for. They fought for a country where people could be committed to their God, country and family. In fighting and giving themselves for such a country, they taught that COMMITMENT to God is the greatest thing that a man can do for himself, his family and his country. But today most people do not even understand the definition of the word "commitment."

May I share with you a story that might help you understand what commitment is all about? The story begins one day when a Chicken and a Hog were walking through town on the sidewalk. As they walked pass a church building they noticed the Sunday morning sermon posted on the sign, "Helping the Poor". Noticing the sign the Chicken came up with a suggestion. "Say, brother Hog, why don't we give all the poor people in town a nice breakfast of Ham and Eggs?" The Hog thought a moment and then replied, "That's all right for you to say, because for you it's only a contribution, but for me, it's a total commitment."

You see, the problems with our society, would be solved if we had less chickens, making contributions and more Men and Women making and keeping commitments. When Men and Women realize relationships are built on more than one night stands and are willing to stand before God and vow their love to each other from the heart for life. When Men and Women realize that children are a gift from God, and that as He gives us these precious gifts, He expects us to give more than just a contribution of ourselves to them. When you and I commit ourselves to our companions, to our children, and to our God, we will began to see the Home reestablished as a place of Love, the church as a place Worship, Schools as a place of obtaining true knowledge, and our Country would return to be a Country that is respected rather than scorned.

God has blessed us with another beautiful day, but so many will not enjoy it because they are not committed to the One and only true God, which is the only relationship that will bring true joy and peace to their lives. When Christ was asked what was the greatest commandment, meaning the greatest thing that we should be committed to. He replied, "And you shall love the Lord your God with all your heart, with all your soul, with all your mind, and with all your strength. This is the first commandment. And the second, like it, is this: 'You shall love your neighbor as yourself. There is no other command- ment greater than these" Mark 12:30 - 31 (NKJV). Because once a person loves God with all his heart and his neighbor, they then are committed to God and the laws of God will come naturally.

Paul seemed to clearly understand this principal of truth as he closed his letter to the church of Corinth by saying, "All the brethren greet you. Greet one another with a holy kiss.. . .If anyone does not love the Lord Jesus Christ, let him be accursed. O Lord, come! The grace of our Lord Jesus Christ be with you" 1 Corinthians 16:20 - 23 (NKJV).

Why not allow this day to become a wonderful day as God intended it. Commit all that you are to Him. When we truly give ourselves, our chil- dren and all that is dear to us to God, He will bless our homes and this country as he did Abraham in Genesis 22:1-19.

In Hot Water

We now live in a world, where the cost of fuel has now gone way beyond anything that we could have ever imagined, and there seems to be no end in sight, which has now changed the cost of food, utilities and entertainment, things which we had begun to believe were pleasures that were owed to us because we are Americans, to now becoming items that we have to choose wisely. In the midst of all this, we now see that we have become a people not of action as our forefathers were, but a people who complain and ask, "What is the government going to do about our problems?" We have forgotten that we are a nation built upon "Free Enterprise" not socialism, or communism, but where "Supply and Demand" is the greatest regulators of value. In other words the fastest way to lower the cost of fuel would be for us to cut our usage in half immediately, both individually and commercially (Drastic times call for drastic measures). If we would stop complaining about the foreign oil rich nations bringing us to our knees and fight back as our forefathers would have by buckling our belts tighter, we could bring them to their knees, as they would have a surplus that nobody would want.

My dad once told me an illustration that he had another preacher tell. He said there was a daughter who complained to her father about her life and how things were so hard for her. She made the statement that she did not know how she was going to make it and felt as though she should just give up. Her father, who was a chef by trade, took her to his kitchen. He then proceeded to fill three pots with water and then placed each pot on a high flame. Soon the pots of water began to boil. As the daughter watched she noticed that he begin to place only one item in each pot. In the first pot he placed a carrot, in the second he placed an egg, and in the last one he placed a coffee bean. He then let them sit and boil without saying a word. The daughter sucked her teeth and impatiently waited, wondering what in the world is he doing? In about twenty minutes he turned off the burners and proceeded to fish out the carrot and the egg and placed each in a bowl. Lastly he poured the coffee in a bowl.

Turning to his daughter he asked, "Darling, what do you see?" to which she replied "A carrot, an egg and coffee". Then he brought her closer and asked her to feel the carrot. She did and noted that it was soft. He then asked her to take the egg and break it. As she followed his instructions of pulling off the shell, she observed that the egg was now hard-boiled. Finally, he asked her to sip the coffee. As she did she smiled and asked, "What does it mean, father?" He then explained that each of the items had faced the same adversity, boiling water, but each had reacted differently. The carrot went in strong, hard and unrelenting. But after being subjected to the boiling water, it softened and became weak. The egg had been fragile with a thin outer shell that protected its liquid inside. But after enduring the boiling water, its inside had become hardened. The coffee bean however was unique. As it was subjected to the heat of the boiling water, it changed the water. As they took note of these changes he then asked his daughter, "Which are you? When adversity knocks on your door, how do you respond? Are you a carrot, an egg or a coffee bean?"

As I say so often, let's bring this thought home to you and me, which are you? Are you more like the carrot, which seems to be hard and strong, yet when pain and problems come your way, do you wilt and become soft and lose your strength? Or are you like the egg, which starts out with a malleable heart and a fluid spirit, but after a death, a breakup, a divorce, or a layoff, have you become hardened and stiff? Your shell may look the same but inwardly you are bitter and tough with a stiff spirit and heart! Or can you say that you are like the coffee bean? Instead of the bean being changed by the boiling hot water, the bean changed the water. Instead of changing and becoming weak or hard, the bean took the pain and as the water got hotter, it just added a better taste to that which was affecting it. If we become like the coffee bean, when things are their worst, we can get better and make things better around us.

As life may get difficult to handle and understand, does our praises to the Lord increase? When the hour is the darkest and the trials are their greatest, does our worship elevate to another level? This is a good illustration and a very good way to look at ourselves. How do we handle conflict, trouble and all types of problems as they come our way? Are you a carrot, an egg, or a coffee bean?

2 Corinthians 4:8-9, reads, "*We are* hard pressed on every side, yet not crushed; *we are* perplexed, but not in despair; persecuted, but not forsaken; struck down, but not destroyed." So whatever hardship that you may be facing today, look to Jesus and ask how you can use this opportunity to change the world around you, that it might glorify Him and bring peace and hope to others and yourself. For with His strength we can turn that Lemon into Lemon-aide.

You Have a Friend

We live in a very blessed time here in America. Who would have ever dreamed that we would see people putting gasoline that cost over $3.00 a gallon in vehicles that cost more than $20,000 each and most households have more than one, living in homes that are valued for more than $100,000 while constantly on the road traveling to be entertained. It is mind boggling. Yet at the same time as you listen to the conversations of these same people all you hear are complaints about everything and blaming everybody for everything that is wrong in the world around them. Every week it seems someone has gone into a School, Mall or Church and rapidly killed as many people as they could before killing themselves, while suicide and divorce seems to have touched every family, and on top of all that, prisons can't be built fast enough to house the people who need to be taken out of society because of the anger and attitude that is sweeping the country. There seems to be something void in the lives of people whom God chose to live in this very blessed land and day.

During my prayer and devotional time this morning one of the things I read to allow the Lord to speak to me was "Open Windows" published by LifeWay. Many of you probably also read it as Schuyler Peterson reminded us of the amazing lives of Helen Keller and Anne Sullivan. I hope most of you know their story. Peterson wrote, "As Helen became blind and deaf at the age of 19 months, but through the tutelage of Anne, Helen became a remarkable example of how a motivated physically impaired person can accomplish greater things than most 'whole' people. As Anne and Helen toured the world together, demonstrating Helen's skills to educators, people sometimes asked if she yearned to have her sight back. Helen would answer, 'I'd rather walk in the dark with a friend than walk in the light alone.'" It seems that the deaf and blind Helen Keller found the void that so many who have so much, do not have, a friend, a true friend.

It is very true, we live in a time when people have more toys, and more time than they know what to do with, but yet at the same they are busy being busy. And yes we all know a lot of people; we have acquaintances, but not friends. The wise Solomon tells us why we need friends and why there is void in our life without them. Solomon tells us that "A friend loves at all times" Proverbs 17:17 (NKJV), that a friend helps us to become the kind of person we should as they love us in spite of our faults and even lovingly point them out to us to help make us a better person as he says, "As iron sharpens iron, So a man sharpens the countenance of his friend." Proverbs 27:17. And then he brings it all together in Proverbs 18:24 as he tells how that we can fill that void in our life and why we need to as he tells us "A man *who has* friends must himself be friendly, But there is a friend *who* sticks closer than a brother."

Ms Helen Keller had a great friend in Ms Anne Sullivan, but being a friend Sullivan introduced Keller to the greatest friend of all, which sealed their friendship for eternity, Jesus Christ, The Son of God. We know according to Luke 7:34 and Matthew 11:19, Christ desires to be your friend, no matter who you are, as Christ was called the friend of Sinners, tax collectors, winebibbers and gluttons. Just as Abraham was known as the friend of God because he believed and it was accounted to him for righteousness, (Luke 7:34) so can you. It is true; you have a friend in Him. And I believe as you build that friendship, as it begins to fill that great void in your life, He will lead you into other friendships such as Helen and Anne had. Friends that are not only friends for now, but friends that will be friends for all eternity, because of the Great Friend they have in common.

Head Turners

If you've seen me around town lately, you've seen the red 1965 Mustang that I been working on for some time now. Many of the people who have seen it have said, "Oh I've always wanted one of those" or "I used to have a mustang like that..." then they begin to remember when, and usually try to remember why they don't have it anymore. Often we forget, not only do we change, but things change, and we think we've got to have something else. While it's true I have a fascination for mostly older cars, I can't afford but one at a time. So there comes the time to sell and buy, because I get a lot of joy in working on them and watching them change, from what they were, to what I dreamed they could become.

I first began to love the older cars just before I turned seventeen. You see, when I turned sixteen I had saved up enough money ($800) to buy a 1967 Buick Wild Cat Convertible, but that was in 1972. Just before I was to turn seventeen, I thought I was in the market for a new car. While shopping, I spotted a 1951 Ford Coupe sitting on a lot. I forgot about the new car, kept my Buick and bought the Ford, which my family nick-named "Old Henry". I enjoyed driving "Old Henry" for eleven years. As young people do, I eventually fell in love with a beautiful girl, who happens to be the only girl I ever let ride in "Old Henry", because they were both very special to me. But after Judy and I married, the boys came along, finances got tight, and "Old Henry" had to go.

Judy has never really understood my fascination with old cars, until about eleven years ago when I had finally finished rebuilding a 1964 Chevrolet Step-side Pick-up. You see, it was about two years earlier that I had decided to sell my nice late model Dodge truck so that I could buy this old 1964 Chevrolet truck that had been sitting in a barn for eighteen years. When I drove it home, it had only one brake and was running on only two cylinders, and was many colors, mostly rust.

After I get one of these old cars, the first I do is to get it drivable, so that I can have a car to drive. But when I first start to drive them, they do not always look drivable. So it was with the Chevrolet truck. Judy would not go anywhere with me in it. Even the elderly ladies at the church asked me to please get rid of it, because they thought it looked bad for their pastor to be driving something that looked that ugly. But about a year and half later, after a lot of elbow grease, new paint, wheels and tires, their attitudes began to change. One day I asked Judy to drive it to work, because I had to do something to her car. She came home smiling, and even allowed me to take her out on a date in it that evening, (she even sat in the middle like she did before children). She now realized it was a classic and enjoyed being seen in it.

That truck now belongs to someone else and there have been others since, such as the Mustang I now drive, that were really not desirable vehicles when I saw them, but they soon became what I call "Head-turners". Though I may not have the vehicle, I still have pictures. Pictures of what it was, and what I saw it could be and became. I share this thought with you, because I think God is like that with us. We think and see ourselves sometimes as useless junk because we have made some wrong decisions in our lives. We may see ourselves as not running on all cylinders and may see ourselves as useless because of the pings and bangs of life and the many colors that have begun to show. But please, be assured that God sees what He intended for us to be, an original, very special classic which He loves and has very special plans for.

The Bible gives us many illustrations of this. In Jeremiah 18:1-6 He refers to God as the Potter and you and me as clay to be molded by His hands. In the analogy of the old cars, you could say, "He is the Master Mechanic able to take our junk and change us into a "Head Turner" that resembles Him", such as He did with men like Moses, David and Gideon. There was a time when people saw Moses as a murderer hiding on the backside of a hill, but God saw a great leader. People saw David as a little shepherd boy, but God saw a King. Gideon seemed to be shy and timid, but God saw a great warrior for his people. When God begins calling you, don't refer to yourself as junk and useless, but begin to allow the Master Mechanic to begin tuning and even sanding on your rough areas. When you allow Him to rebuild and work in your life, others will no longer see junk, but they will begin to see the beauty that He saw. He can take that which we have let deteriorate, and make us new in Him. As He said in 2 Corinthians 5:17, "Therefore, if anyone *is* in Christ, *he is* a new creation; old things have passed away; behold, all things have become new" (NKJV).

As you begin to take a new look at the very special person you are in His sight, also take a new look at your children, friends and companion, and see what God sees. When He allows you to see the beautiful classic that they are, please encourage them to let Christ have His way in their life.

Antiques and Hot Rods

Those who know me well know that I have a passion for old cars and trucks. When I really want to escape and enjoy life, I like to be found at an antique or Hot Rod car show. I can spend hours on hours and never get tired of admiring these beautiful machines. Since those types of shows are few and far between, I have found that I can also be rejuvenatcd by going to our back yard and begin working on (and what I really like is detailing) a project vehicle that I may have at that time. No, neither one of my vehicles is really that outstanding, but they're mine and I can spend hours and feel satisfied that my day has been well spent, because I can look back with pride and see something accomplished for a while. I even enjoy cleaning out and detailing Judy's HHR.

What is really neat is after I have detailed them with a good wax job and put Rain-X on the glass, a rain comes. Because of the preparation and care that has been done before hand, the rain just sheds off, and with a wipe of a chamois cloth it shines like new again.

Even though I really do enjoy working with the older vehicles and the renewed attitude that I seem to get from it, I again realize that those days also do not come as often as I need them. Like you, I find I like to have that kind of feeling everyday. Recently as I shared with someone, I realized that I have also discovered another great way to turn even bad days into bearable and even great days.

Maybe you're not a morning person, as I am. I love my mornings. I have found that after I've showered and dressed, and the family is all doing what they need to be doing, that I can get alone with God and His Word for an hour. I become like that car, waxed and ready for anything.

Of course to start your day with prayer and with the Lord you must have a relationship with Him. If at this point in your life you have never presented yourself to Him to become your Lord and Savior, there is no better time than the present to invite Him into your life. For He is always listening for the sinners' repentance prayer, confessing that you are a sinner in need of Him, to be Lord and Redeemer of your life, because He has promised, "That if thou shalt confess with thy mouth the Lord Jesus, and shalt believe in thine heart that God hath raised him from the dead, thou shalt be saved. For with the heart man believeth unto righteousness; and with the mouth confession is made unto salvation. .... For whosoever shall call upon the name of the Lord shall be saved" (Romans 10:9-13 KJV). As you pray from your heart in faith, you will begin a great new relationship with Him today.

You may say "I don't have an hour in the morning". May I encourage you to begin with designating fifteen minutes? Now please let me share with you why this is worth all this great effort that you are going to have to put forth to have this time with the Lord. First, all of us come into contact with people everyday who feel it is their calling in life to make everyone around them miserable. Without saying a word, but they always do, they destroy all the good intentions you had for the day. Secondly, there is hardly ever a day that goes by that everything goes just as we plan. Whether it's through a person or machinery, a storm blows in and everything becomes chaotic. BUT, I have discovered that when I begin my morning with the Lord, reading His Words that He has for me that day, and praying for my family, friends and even enemies, it seems He puts a good coat of wax on me. Then when the storm of the day comes, that would normally destroy my entire day, it sort of beads up and just rolls off. Then with a "Thank You Lord", He wipes me with the Holy Spirit and I'm refreshed once again, ready for the next storm and a good night's rest.

As you close your eyes tonight, why not plan on starting your new day with "Good Morning, Lord" instead of "Oh Lord, its morning"? You will never regret it, whether you're an Antique, Hot Rod, or even a new modernized model. You can still shine and stand out, because you are a unique creation of the almighty God. Phil 2:15 says: "That ye may be blameless and harmless, the sons of God, without rebuke, in the midst of a crooked and perverse nation, among whom ye shine as lights in the world"

Runs Like A Deer

When we first moved to Chipley ten years ago, the first friends that we made outside the church where we were serving were Max and Sue Laseter. At one point early in our relationship, Max dropped by the church office to see me. In previous conversations he had shared with me about two older vehicles that he had. This time he came by to share with me that Sue wanted the 1969 Ford truck out of the yard, because it had not run in a long time and no one seemed to want to fix it for him. So to make her happy, Max said to me, "If you will come get it out of the yard, I would give you the title." To which I answered, "Thomas and I will be there tomorrow, as soon he gets out of school." And that is what we did and what he did.

From that point on for several weeks, every time I had a spare moment I was working on the old Ford, trying to figure out why it would not run. Early on I came to the conclusion that the motor was froze up, so I began to pour Sea Foam in the crank case, carburetor and gas tank. After a while I guess you could say I became more determined than ever to get it running. I then determined that I would "fix it or break it". I tied the Ford to the back of the Dodge truck that I had just fixed for myself, and told Thomas, our middle son who was sixteen at the time, to begin to pull me through town toward

Wendell Webb's, because I knew if anyone could fix it, he could. But I also told Thomas to forget everything I had ever told him about pulling a vehicle. I said, don't look back and don't stop, no matter how bad it may sound behind you. This time he obeyed, because when we came to the Traffic light at Brickyard road I heard something and tried to get him to stop, but there was no stopping him. Finally by the next traffic light he believed that I did want him to stop and we pulled into the vacant lot at the corner. And sure enough, the old truck was running like a deer, a "John Deere" that is, just as sweet as it could be. From that point on I did a little work to the old truck, had it painted and Thomas drove it to school and work for the next three or four years.

I tell you that story because I'm afraid that is where many of us are in our relationship with Jesus Christ, individually, as the Church and particularly as a nation. We have become so self-centered we do not serve the purpose we were created for. David in Second Samuel sang a song and in it told how the Lord was everything he needed as He made his feet like that of a deer and helped them to be set on high places. The Lord kept them steady as he trusted and served the Lord as the deer trusted its creator (2 Samuel 22:34). And then David's chief Musician wrote in Psalms 42:1, "As the deer pants for the water brooks, so pants my soul for You, O God" (NKJV).

What I see as I look at myself, the condition of the local church and our nation, it seems our souls are seeking everything except God and His holiness in our lives. And at some point I see the Lord looking at us and saying, "I must do, what I must do, 'fix it or break it', so that they can be restored to a vessel that brings honor to Me." After all that is why He created us, and saved us, that through all eternity we could worship and praise Him for Who He is.

For a long time now that has been my prayer, for me, my family and the local church, and now for our nation. "Lord whatever it takes, if it takes breaking us to fix us, so that our soul will pant for You as a deer does for the water, so be it Lord."

Restore the Shine

When reading the life of King David, you will find that he came to a point in his life where he yielded to the flesh rather than turning to the Lord for strength during a time of great temptation. Because of his rejection of God's will for his life, he discovered after Nathan had confronted him, that he had lost the joy of his salvation (Psalm 51:12). Notice the Bible said he lost the joy of his salvation, not his salvation. Everyday it seems I meet people who are basically in the same situation. They will say they know that they are Christians, but by witnessing their life there seems to be no evidence of joy there. You see, as David found out, the real joy of our salvation comes from the relationship that we have with our Lord. But when we have chosen to follow after the flesh, that relationship begins to deteriorate, and the joy of that relationship fades.

As you read Psalm 51 you will hear the heart of David as he realizes what he has lost, as he begins to repent and ask the Lord to wash and restore him to that which he once had, realizing that it is the Lord who must do the work in him. I began to get a clearer view of this as I began to work on the latest project that I've started working on in my spare time. Recently I purchased 1983 Jeep Scrambler which had basically been parked in a garage for about 15 years. Because it was not doing that which it was made to do for the last 15 years, parts of it has began to deteriorate, and it has lost some of its appeal and shine. Why it was parked I don't know, probably something broke and the owner lost interest, but I saw something in that Jeep that others may not have seen.

It also reminds me of the same people that David reminded me of. Those who have lost that joy of their salvation and the luster in their life has been lost because of selfish sin. They have also become comfortable, and now as that joy continues to deteriorate they also resist the change that must come about to restore them. That's why the Lord must bring the change as He does the cleaning. It will take a lot of work and time to restore this old Jeep, made by American Motors, back to that which the builder and the original owner enjoyed, but it is possible. It will also take time and willingness on your part for the Lord to work in your life so that you can once again enjoy the fullness of the joy of His salvation, but as you yield to the cleansing work of Christ, it is possible. As I have a desire for this Jeep to be restored to its formal shining, working condition, the Lord has a desire for you to be restored or reconciled to the joy that you once had in Him. The aim of God is to restore man to a dynamic, vital relationship with Him. For Man is most fully human when fulfilling the intention of God for Him, which is: Worshiping, Serving and Loving God our Creator and Redeemer. Of all God's creations, only man has been given this blessed privilege and this is where real joy comes from.

You can experience the wonderful blessings the Lord has for you by simply bringing all your junk and all the things that you have messed up and give them to the Lord as you repent of the sins in your life, or you can continue to resist and continue to deteriorate, and never again experiencing the joy of His Salvation. 2 Corinthians 5:17-21 reads, "Therefore, if anyone *is* in Christ, *he is* a new creation; old things have passed away; behold, all things have become new. Now all things *are* of God, who has reconciled us to Himself through Jesus Christ, and has given us the ministry of reconciliation, that is, that God was in Christ reconciling the world to Himself, not imputing their trespasses to them, and has committed to us the word of reconciliation. Now then, we are ambassadors for Christ, as though God were pleading through us: we implore *you* on Christ's behalf, be reconciled to God. For He made Him who knew no sin *to be* sin for us, that we might become the righteousness of God in Him. (NKJV)"

The Salvage Yard

Most people get excited in anticipation of a New Year. We like to think that because it's a New Year we've got a clean slate to work from. But the opposite is actually true, because we carry all our mistakes, hurts, pains, disappointment and even the bills that we had in the previous year into the new one. The sad fact is that it doesn't take us very long to realize that all our dreams and hopes that the New Year would bring, are actually just that, hopes and dreams.

Though many made resolutions, which you have probably already broken, let me share one with you that will be very beneficial. It's very simple; it is simply submitting yourself to be yielded to be the person that Christ would have you be. Maybe the following analogy will help you understand the benefit of yielding yourself to His will.

To share this I will have to share something personal with you. I like old cars. I like to go to car shows, and I like to fix up old cars that others have thrown aside. So that means I like to go to what we call in the Mountains, Junk Yards. Some of you may call them Wrecking Yards and some even call them Auto Graveyards. But actually the most appropriate way to describe these places would be to call them Salvage Yards. Because the cars are not actually junk, they may be wrecked, but no one is actually going to wreck them again. They are not like the human bodies that have been put in the grave, because you see, there is nothing that we as humans can do to change the decaying process of the body in the grave. But to that auto that's been put aside for one reason or another, there is something that can be done. So it's not actually an Auto Graveyard, but more or less a Salvage Yard.

Myself and many other people enjoy going to the Salvage Yards, or just getting cars that people have shoved to the back yard for twenty or so years, and spend a little time, money and elbow grease, for the joy of seeing these vehicles transformed, often to more elegant vehicles than they were when they were first built. I wish I had the time to tell you about some of these cars and trucks. Of how bad they looked to begin with, and how sharp they were, when we got through with them. The funny thing is, usually when I bring them home and start driving and working on them, my wife and some friends don't want to admit they know me. But once it becomes a showpiece, they get excited for an invitation just to ride through town.

With that thought in mind, let's be honest and take a good look at ourselves, and the way that God may see us. As He looks at us, could He also see a salvage yard, and would love the opportunity to show others what He sees in us? If we would be truthful, we would have to admit that we have failed, because we have tried to control others and ourselves, thus turning ourselves into wrecks of our former selves. So actually the New Year offers very little hope, because of the baggage, that we carry into it. But the Lord says it doesn't have to be that way. If we are willing to yield ourselves to His control as He walks through the salvage yard, for He offers to make us new, again (2 Corinthians 5:17-21).

As you read 2 Corinthians 5:17-21 you will notice a reoccurring word, "Reconciliation" which means; "Someone or something is completely altered and adjusted to a required standard". To put this in simple "Tim Hall terms", God is saying that if we will yield to His masterful hand, He will recycle us so that we might become what He intended for us to be. No, He does not change, but He changes us, that we might have a relationship with Him. He makes in us a new creation, with a new tongue, heart and a new commandment to love one another. In doing so He takes old hurtful parts away and restores them with those that edify Him (Galatians 6:15; Mark 16:17; John 13:34; Ephesians 4:17-32; Colossians 3:1-25; Hebrews 10:20-26). He even gives us a new name and a new home (Revelation 2:17; 21:1-9).

Remember the old cars that have been restored. One thing I have learned is that the job is never finished. As long as it is exposed to the air and elements, and as long as I enjoy it by driving it, which I will, it will get scratched, maybe dented and parts will wear out again. And I will just have to enjoy repairing it over and over again, because

I have never seen a car that can repair itself. The same is true with you and I. As long as we are in this world, even with the new spirit living within us, we will have spiritual battles that will continue until we receive our new body. Paul knew this, and had the same struggle as he confessed he had to die daily to the yielding of the masterful hand of his Lord. So until that day when all things become new, yield all that is within you to Him. If you will, you will enjoy the New Year and the New You as you share His love with others and encourage them to also be yielded to His masterful hands (2 Peter 3:13-14

A Free Car

Every young man has a car that they dream of, but will probably never own. But just imagine that someone drove that car up into your drive, got out, came over to you and handed you the keys and the title with your name on it. This person just says to you, "Because I love you, I am giving you this car." That would be awesome, wouldn't it? I'm sure you would take the car for a ride through town, showing off the car and share how wonderful the person was who gave you the car. But eventually you would need some gas, right and because the car was a free gift, it should not cost you anything, right? You would drive up to the gas pumps and tell the attendant just to put gas in it, because the car was a gift. And then about 3,000 miles down the road, the oil would need changing or the motor will eventually freeze up. And of course that should be free too, because the car is a gift and gifts are free. And even after a while it would get dirty, but since it was free, you should not have to put forth your effort to clean it, should you?

The truth is, though this car was free with no strings attached, in order to drive and enjoy it, you will have to put gas in it, change the oil when needed and even clean it out from time to time. Or you will be riding around with your friends in their cars, driving by yours and waving at it, because it will be useless to you. But it was free, without any strings attached; the car is yours. But unless you do the things necessary to keep it running, it becomes nothing more than a monument to metal and human design in your yard.

This free car illustration was an illustration that Mark Long, professor of New Testament at the Baptist College of Florida used during our Winter Bible Study to help people understand the free gift of Salvation. Since it was an illustration involving a dream car, if you've read me long enough, you know I had to share it. My dream car at this point in life would be something that would be sporty, stand out and shout "This is Tim Hall," maybe an old Studebaker Hawk, a Plymouth Prowler, or a GTX convertible. No matter what it was, as long as it was free, you better believe I would take great care of it. It would never lack for gas, oil or tires and it would be show ready at all times. And when I had a chance to share about the person who gave me the car, you better believe I would always have something good to say.

But actually I have received many gifts that are a lot more valuable and more precious to me than a car. The greatest of these gifts is the gift that Jesus Christ purchased with His life, my salvation. Since the age of 12, when I received this wonderful gift, which I did not deserve and there was no way that I could ever earn it or be able to purchase it, I have treasured it. And because of my love and appreciation for this wonderful gift, which was free without any strings, I take great pride in taking care of my testimony/witness so that I do not bring shame to Him. I get up and read my Bible and spend an hour with my Lord every morning. Not because I have to, but because I desire to, because of the relationship we have, and that I want that relationship to grow. I go to church, Bible studies, and participate in out-reach from our church. Not because I have to in order to maintain my salvation, but if I didn't, my salvation would be nothing more than an unnoticed monument sitting in the corner. But because of my appreciation and love of the person who has given me this awesome gift, I'm going to keep it fueled and clean that others may see Him through me, and therefore they will glorify Him and even desire to receive the gift which He has for them.

Tell you the truth, I have a very hard time believing that people who only attend church a few times a year, or even once a week, people who are always making excuses about their language, attitude and church attendance, have anything more than a church membership, but that's my opinion. I agree that standing in a garage will not make you a car and attending church does not make one a saint. But it's about as close as you are going to get to one, till you receive His gift, and begin to let Him shine through you. Remember that John 3:16 says, "For God so loved the world, that he gave his only begotten Son, that whosoever <u>believeth</u> in him should not perish, but have everlasting life" (KJV). And remember the word "believe" in that scripture is not talking about head knowledge, but is talking about giving your allegiance to Him above all things, allowing Him to be Lord of all in your life.

You see, with the gift of Salvation, just as with the free car, with it come responsibilities, If you've received eternal life through Jesus Christ and His righteousness, don't let it sit on the couch like some monument to an unknown God. Keep it fueled with His word and cleansed through daily repentance and so that you grow in your walk and that others may desire the gift that He has purchased for them. He is my reason to rejoice and live, and He can be yours.

Maintenance Required

As I write, I am making plans to be at one of my favorite places, Spence Field in Moultrie Georgia, for the bi-annual Swap-Meet and Car Show. Normally I go just to look and dream, but this time I have something I would like to sell. But I'm sure I will get lost in a dream or two of a classic that I would like to give a good home.

Most of the classic automobiles that I've owned, I have driven on a daily basis, which is not the normal thing to do. Most of the time if you own a classic, the only times they come out of the garage are for a show. Of course, the ones that I have owned have not been your high dollar cars, just ones that made good conversation pieces. But no matter how costly an old car may or may not be, they all demand attention, or they will let you down on the road.

I'm taking what we call a 39 Ford Coupe Cargo trailer, which we have enjoyed pulling behind my PT Cruiser when we travel for the past few years. It has made our travel much more interesting and enjoyable because of the attention it draws, but it's time to move on and liquidate, so that Judy will have money to spend on me for Valentine's. That's right, men, Valentine's Day is just around the corner, and the truth is, I don't really care if I get anything, but I know a special lady who does.

It is true, men and women are made differently, and it's not all on the exterior that we are different, but we are wired differently. Sounds like I'm talking about cars again. Maybe that's a good idea. Most of us guys take a lot of pride in ours cars, trucks and bikes and even spend a lot of time with them to keep them in good shape, because when we get a chance to show them off, we want them to perform well and look good. Now ladies, don't get too upset when you figure out where I am going with this. But sometimes, to get something over to the men, you just have to talk their language.

Ok, guys, you have to admit it, we have a tendency to really go all out when we want to entice that pretty girl that we set our eyes on. But once that ring's on her finger, we forget that she requires maintenance. When you said "I do", you agreed to love, honor and cherish her for the rest of your life. And to put things in a simple perspective, that's what it will take to have a happy marriage.

Think about it this way, when we do get a new truck or a classic car, we enjoy them for a while, then about three years down the road, they come out with a new design, or we spot a more classic model and we're ready to do some trading. Very few men keep a car more than three or four years. If they do, they begin to do some major restoration to it, and then they keep it another three or four years. Remember, when you married your wife, the dream of your life, you promised her, her family and God, that you would cherish her for the rest of your life. But as humans go, after about three years, we get in a rut, and other things began to get our attention. Well, just like with cars, if you give her a little more personal attention, she will brighten your world once again. Besides, you know what you have, but when you go trading, you don't know what you may be getting (now, be nice, Tim).

Most of us watch that little sticker that's in the corner of the windshield, to make sure our cars get the attention they need at the proper times. Well, there are also little stickers in marriage that we need to pay attention to, so that our marriage gets the proper maintenance that it needs. Valentine's Day is one of them, along with anniversaries and birthdays, etc... It's not necessarily about expensive gifts, but about focusing on the person, that is important to you, and letting her know it. No matter how long you've been married, a date with your companion is one of the greatest marriage maintenance tools there is, and it will bring out the shine in both of you.

Remember, she is wired different. Don't waste your time trying to figure that out. Just remember to admire her with your eyes and words as you did when you first met, and she will be proud to shine for you, and be there when you need her. If you give her the attention you would a pricey, classic car, she won't let you down, though the car may. Also remember what I've shared with you for many years, "What every woman wants is to be treated like a Queen, by a man who deserves to be treated like a King". It's God's perfect plan (Ephesians 5:22-25).

To the Queen of our Home, the love of my life and my best friend, Happy Valentine's, Judy, I love you.

Happy Anniversary

Thirty-one years ago on June Seventh, Judy and I stood before a group composed of family, friends, and God, in the front of a church on a hill in north Georgia and said "I do". That's actually an amazing accomplishment in the day in which we live, especially considering that we went steady for three years prior to that day, and considering that she was only fifteen and I was seventeen when we began to date and that we lived over thirty miles from each other.

So how in this world have we been able to accomplish this, still dreaming and planning and looking forward to years down the road, considering that in many ways we are different: She's laid back, easy going and a very likeable person, while I'm hyper-active, anxious and maybe not so likeable according to some people. She enjoys working and spending time on the computer, but to me they are part of my job. I like being out piddling with old cars, while her only concern for a car is, "will it get me where I want to go and back?" I always thought I would marry a red head and she's a blonde. As a young person she said she would never be married to a preacher. She likes to stay home and I like to go. So you see it is an amazing accomplishment considering that one out of every two marriages in our generation has not survived.

Do you notice I used the word "survived" and not the "D" word? That's one of the reasons right there. We agreed when we married that the "D" word did not exist; it would never be in our vocabulary. You see we replaced that word with another word which is very important to us "commitment". That's the first key to a happy, successful marriage after love.

Yes, I was struck on her the first time I saw her, even though she had a boy friend at that time and was with him, and was not a red head. I did not speak to her that time but three months later, they had broke up and her family visited my family and as soon I could talk with her I let her know my attraction for her (actually stole a kiss, I know shame on me). But our history began with that kiss. And yes, we had some rocky days while dating and in our marriage, but that attraction became love and that love grew and continues to grow stronger.

Our commitment was sealed as we made a covenant with each other before God and our families. So considering that we are stuck together, with no way out; so what do you do? Enjoy life together, make the best out of it, love the God that brought us together and love each other with all that is in us, and talk. Matter-of-fact, talk a lot and listen a lot, it's called communication.

What's the secret to being happily married? Allow your love to grow for each other until it actually becomes adoration for each other and the things that are different about you. Be committed to each other even though that has become a bad word in the world we live in. And communicate, communicate, communicate, for you have no better friend than the love of your life, and with your best friend, there are no secrets.

To you who are reading this today, may you also have a blessed and wonderful marriage! To Judy, Happy Anniversary, and as they say on birthdays, may we have many more! Love you!

Being A Screwdriver

Let me ask you a question, how many screwdrivers do you have around your place and what do you do with them? If you are like we are, we have screwdrivers everywhere. Judy, my wife, keeps one in a kitchen drawer, each desk has one, end tables have one, night stands may have one and each tool box has more screwdrivers than any other tool. It seems that a screwdriver is always close by and handy to use. And you would think the answer to what you use a screwdriver for would be simply to screw or unscrew a screw. But if the truth be known, a screwdriver is used for many more things and most the time for others things other than what they were designed for, because they are so handy and available to be used. Here are just a few things that I have used a screwdriver for: to pry with, to dig with, to scrape a surface with, as a measuring tape, as a straight edge, as a hammer, an oil filter wrench, as pliers to hold a bolt, a bottle or can opener; you name it, I think I have tried to do it with a screwdriver. Why, because it was the closest tool when I needed a tool.

We live in a time when many believers make excuses to why they are not participating in some type of ministry through the local church and why they themselves have not been a part of introducing someone else to Christ, even though the Great

Commission (Matthew 28:18-20; Mark 16:15; Acts 1:7-8) commands it of those who are His followers. The reason many fail to be all that the Lord had planned for them is because we have come to believe, like doctors, that we are specialists, specializing in one area. With that idea a person will specialize in one area such as teaching, music, etc., and then expect others to do evangelism, thinking they have done their part, even though they have not. Then others think that they don't know enough to share or are afraid that their testimony does not bare witness of what they need to share.

In Second Corinthians 11:5-6 Paul said that he considered himself inferior to others apostles, even untrained in speech, yet he knew that God had given him knowledge because of his experiences, which were manifested in his life because of his walk with Christ. Basically what Paul was saying is "I'm like a screwdriver; I'm available, close by and God has used me, though I may not be the perfect tool. Availability, handy and useable are wonderful values when placed in the Master's hands."

This past week as I began to look over things that I am thankful for in my life, I came to realize that when I was fifteen I began to desire a close walk with my Lord, and because of that decision He has allowed me to be like a screwdriver in His hands. And I praise the Lord for that, because if I had not, even though I might have been the best tool for the job, He could have reached for one that was closer to Him and used them instead, and they would have received many of the blessings that I have. No, like Paul, I may not be the best speaker, writer or tool that He had in His box for the job, but I am thankful that He chose to use me because I was close, available and useable in His hands.

I've always encouraged others and have strived in my life, to set my goals so high that I know that I can't reach them by myself, but with His help, reach for that goal so that He will be glorified through my life (Isaiah 40:31; Philippians 4:11). Basically by looking back I can say, I praise the Lord that I have been a screwdriver in His hands and hopefully always will be. And I hope you also can see yourself as a tool He can use to bring glory and honor to His Holy name, Jesus Christ. For He is not only the reason for the season, He is the reason for All things and is worthy of our praise and worship by the life that we live. (Ephesians 5:15-21 Colossians 3:12-25).

Transformers

B randon, our nine year old grandson, spent a few days with us the week before the Fourth. On our hour journey to the house from Tallahassee, all he could talk about was the new movie that was coming out, July the Fourth, "Transformers". While traveling and listening to him talk, Judy, my wife, seemed to remember that twenty or so years ago when our boys were young, that the first "Transformers" movie came out, and she seemed to think that we had that original movie somewhere. We both knew that our boys at one time had a lot of those "Transformer" toys. And sure enough as we began to pull things from storage, she found the movie. Of course, the first older movie was a cartoon style movie, while I understand that the new, 2007 movie has real people and real cars and trucks in it. Also I heard this morning on the news that it brought in millions of dollars last week, the highest of all the movies out. I probably will not see the new movie till it comes out on video and one of the kids rent or buy it and bring it to the house. By watching the new Chevrolet commercials which features "Transformers" and the old movie, I have an idea of the plot and what the movie is about (I don't know, but does this prove "that there is nothing new under the Sun". OK, as my friend Bill Burtoft keeps telling me, I'm getting out there, so I'll come back to earth).

Basically for those who don't know, and have never seen either movie or played with a transformer toy, "Transformers" are basically robots who have been given life by a source of life, and they can reconfigure themselves into two or three different configurations, such as: being a sharp shiny sports car it travels down the road at high rates of speed, but as it jumps a hill it transforms itself into a large robot which stands upon two legs, with arms, a head and usually some type of awesome weaponry with which it seeks to protect civilization from the evil transformers which may be an airplane that transforms into an equally strong robot as the other. To say the least, it's a transforming battle between good and evil.

Actually, I sort of get tired of people always trying to take things which are secular and try to turn it into something spiritual, but this one, just because of the name of the movie, I must reflect upon this it. By that I mean, in the movie, "Transformers" these robots transform from one very useful machine such as a car or plane, into a robot or some type of war machine for another purpose that the first machine could not accomplish except for the transformation. Then they transform back to the original and so forth.

You probably have all ready figured out where I'm going with this. Many, many years ago when

I was twelve, in a mission on the North side of Chicago, just blocks from Wrigley Field, I was transformed from a boy without any hope or purpose to a new creation in Christ (2 Corinthians 5:17), with a new and exciting purpose and reason to live. And the beautiful part of this transformation is that I will never transform back to that which I was (Romans 8:38-39). And since then I have had the wonderful opportunity to witness many people, who where enslaved by alcohol, drugs, sexual immoralities, anger, rotten attitudes, deceptiveness, gambling, depression, etc. set free and transformed for eternity, never to return to that which they once were, because when the Holy Spirit takes up residence in an individual, Christ becomes Lord of all they are, while His Word from the Bible becomes their guide for life. They are transformed with a testimony of deliverance and given a new peace and hope because of the relationship they now have with God which He has been sealed with the blood of His Son Jesus Christ upon a cruel Roman cross.

Oh yes, and because of the first transformation that took place when I repented of my sin by turning to and trusting Christ, one day I know that a more glorious transformation will take place when Christ returns for His bride, the true church, as I will receive a new body such as Christ had after His resurrection from the grave (1 Corinthians 15:51-58; The Revelation of Jesus Christ 21:1-5).

If you have not experienced the first transformation as I did at the age of twelve, I hope that you will very soon, by simply confessing "with your mouth the Lord Jesus and believe in your heart that God has raised Him from the dead, you will be saved. For with the heart one believes unto righteousness, and with the mouth confession is made unto salvation" (Romans 10:9-10 NKJV).

Transformation

One of the most popular things to be included in movies and cartoons in the past twenty years is a thing called "transformation." A young man runs into a phone booth and is transformed into Super Man, another leaves his home through an elevator that takes him down deep into a cave where he is transformed into Batman. Others through different means are transformed into Spider Man, the Hulk, and so forth. On a cartoon called the transformers, cars and boats are transformed into unimaginable fighting machines to save the world, and then there's the unforgettable Mighty Mouse and Under Dog. Then you have the more recent movies taken from the old standbys like Charlie's Angels where a man is able to train and develop women who can walk on walls and take on an army of men.

Hollywood may think they have come up with something that challenges the imagination of the mind, but the truth is, transformation of "man" has been taking place long before Hollywood was even thought of. Jesus Christ has been transforming the lives of people who were worthless and useless, as society would refer to them, into people who have made a great difference in this world. I was just reading of such a person who God changed in an article written by Derl Keefer in "Preaching Now." His article reminded me of the day that I was seated behind the mike at WDOD-FM in Chattanooga and a man entered the control room and introduced himself as Stuart Hamblen. He handed me a couple of 45's, on which he had recorded himself singing some songs he had written, as he began to tell me his story.

You see, in the 50's Stuart Hamblen was a well known radio host/comedian/song writer in Hollywood, who was also well known for his drinking, womanizing, partying, etc. But one a day a young preacher came, holding a tent revival and Hamblen invited him to his radio show so that he could presumably poke fun at him. So to have plenty of material to use on the young preacher, Hamblen attended the revival meetings.

Early in the service the preacher announced, "There is a man in this audience who is a big fake." Like many others there that night Hamblin was convinced he was talking about him. After the service those words continued to haunt Hamblen until a couple of nights later he showed up drunk at the preacher's hotel door around two in the morning demanding that preacher pray for him! But the preacher refused, saying, "This is between you and God and I'm not going to get in the middle of it." But he did invite him in and they talked till five in the morning, at which point Hamblin dropped to his knees with tears in his eyes, while crying out to God.

At that point God transformed Hamblen, as he quit drinking, and chasing women and all that stuff

his friends thought were fun. Because of his transformation he lost favor with the Hollywood crowd
and was ultimately fired from the radio station
when he refused to accept a sponsorship from a
beer company. From there he tried to write a few
"Christian" songs, but only one which he had written
for a friend, Rosemary Clooney, had much success,
"This Ole House."

Let me continue his story as written by Keffer.
"As he continued to struggle, a long time friend
named John took him aside and told him, 'All your
troubles started when you got religion. Was it worth
it all?' Stuart answered simply, 'Yes.'

"Then his friend asked, 'You liked your booze so
much, don't you ever miss it?' and his answer was
'No.' John then said, 'I don't understand how you
could give it up so easily.'

"And Stuart's response was, 'It's no big secret.
All things are possible with God.' To that John said,
'That's a catchy phrase. You should write a song
about it.'

"And as they say, 'The rest is history.' The song
Stuart wrote was 'It Is No Secret.'

'It is no secret what God can do,
What He's done for others, He'll do for you.
With arms wide open, He'll welcome you,
It is no secret what God can do. . .'

"By the way. . . the friend was John Wayne. And
the young preacher who would not pray for Stuart
Hamblen? That was Billy Graham."

I wish that every one of you had the opportunity that I had to meet Stuart Hamblen, for he was a very super and special man after the Lord transformed him, and that is one of those experiences I will never forget. But though in this life you will not be able to meet Stuart, you can meet the one who transformed his life and He is still in the transforming business (2 Corinthians 5:17; Romans 3:10 & 23; 5:8 & 12; 6:23;10:9-13).

Toothpaste

Why is it that people look for fault in others? Then when they think they have some hot and juicy story on someone else, whether true or not, they tell others. The way I see it, America is in a sad state! Billions of people sit around and watch other people on TV doing the unthinkable with each other. Then when they are not watching these immoral programs they are trying to destroy those around them with outright lies (called gossip). You see, I have always been taught if you didn't **see** it happen, then you actually don't **know** it happened. So the truth is you could be repeating a lie if you repeat it. I have also been taught and taught my children, "Never believe what you hear and only half of what you see."

So many of these lies get started because two people are having an innocent conversation and someone who doesn't have a life, tells a lie to someone else, who tells it to someone else, who tells it to someone else, etc. It seems to me that there are a lot of people who need to get a life and they need a personal experience with Jesus Christ.

The sad truth is, most of these who are involved in these lies are local church members. But please don't judge "His Church" by church members who have their name on the local church roll. You see, those who have their names on "His Roll in Heaven" don't have time to talk about other people, because they are excited and talking about Christ and how He is changing their lives.

Most of these busy bodies, which seem to not have a life and like to destroy others, I'm afraid don't really understand the damage they do to others and themselves. My Dad once shared with me about an article he read in the "Focus on the Family" magazine, which is a very good example. It went something like this. A father sat his children down to a table with a tube of toothpaste. He then asks them to get all the toothpaste out of the tube and put it on the table. After they had accomplished that simple task he then laid a $10.00 bill on the table and said, "the first one to put the toothpaste back in the tube could have the ten bucks." He did all this to illustrate to his children something adults never seem to learn. After words come out of the mouth, they can never return. It only takes a small match to destroy a great forest or a large city, and it only takes a little tongue to destroy an individual for life.

So please do everyone a favor, sit on your tongue and read His words. **James 3:3-12; Luke 6:45; Proverbs 15:28; Ephesians 4:29.** If you can't say something good about someone else, why say anything?

By the way, if you listen, it might surprise you, to what others are saying about you. Instead of spreading gossip, try something new, like sharing a smile and the News that Christ has come to seek and to save, and that by the signs, He could return to take "The Church" out today.

Caution Light

Recently Judy and I made a trip to England to visit our oldest son, Steven and his family. As we expected, the main difference that we would notice would be the "driving." Not only do they put the steering wheels on the wrong side of the cars and drive on the wrong side of the road, their signage is poor and roads narrow with no shoulders. And they have those turnabouts that I wrote about a few weeks back. There was one other thing that I found very interesting about the way they control their traffic flow, it was their traffic lights.

In the country side you see very few, if any, traffic lights, just turnabouts. But in the city you would come upon some traffic lights. I never thought that traffic lights could be different, but they are. First of all they seem to be larger than ours and they are not suspended over the lane in which you are driving. Instead they are mounted to a fairly short pole which sits on the white line on the road. Remember the roads are narrow, and now you stick a large metal pole with an even larger light on it, in the middle of the road. The problem really comes when there is more than one lane going each way. You will just have to imagine with me a very narrow road with three lanes going each way and six to ten traffic lights sitting in the middle of a congested intersection. And the light to which you adjust your driving by is the one, well; your guess is as good as mine.

But the real difference about their traffic light is the yellow light, the light we call the caution light. Not only does the caution or yellow light come on as the green light is turning red, but also while the red light is turning green. Most of understand that when the green light goes off and the yellow light comes on, that we should either proceed with caution, or prepare to stop. Well, do you know what you do when you're sitting at a red light in England and the red light goes off and the yellow light comes on? If you're the car or bicycle that is in the front under the light, you get gone, because if you don't, you will get run over. Oh I had forgot to tell you about bicycles in England, they have to obey the same traffic laws as motorist, except they have the right of way at all times, and they get first place at the traffic light (and that is in middle of the road). But still whether you are a car, taxi, bike or bus, if you are on the front line and the red light turns yellow, SCAT, get gone! Things are happening behind you, traffic is moving forward.

As I look around me, at the world situation, and I look in the Bible, I see that God has a traffic light to direct us. It's been glowing crimson red for two thousand years or so, but it is now glowing bright yellow, and will soon turn green.

Over two thousand years ago the world was stopped in its tracks as the sinless Lamb of God, was cruelly crucified upon a crude wooden cross. On that day thousands of years of prophesy were fulfilled, God's amazing, loving grace was extended to everyone that would receive it. While upon the earth, Christ expounded upon the prophesies of Daniel, Ezekiel, Jeremiah and others and promised before He ascended to Heaven, that He would return in like manner for His Bride, the Church. But with that Christ, Paul the apostle, John the Revelator and others told us what the time would be like when He would return (Luke 21). As I have mentioned in previous articles, I believe it is time to pay attention to things that are happening around you and around the world, and read your Bible. As you do, you will notice that for the believer, the disciple of Christ, the red light has turned yellow and soon will be green as Christ will soon say to His bride, "It's time to go, time to leave this world and take up your abode in a new city that I have prepared for you, while I deal with all who have rejected My grace" (please excuse me paraphrasing). I believe it's time for us to get out of the way, so that others can see Him high and lifted up.

Paul said, "This know also, that in the last days perilous times shall come. For men shall be lovers of their own selves, covetous, boasters, proud, blasphemers, disobedient to parents, unthankful, unholy, Without natural affection, trucebreakers, false accusers, incontinent, fierce, despisers of those that are good, Traitors, heady, highminded, lovers of pleasures more than lovers of God; Having a form of godliness, but denying the power thereof: from such turn away. For of this sort are they which creep into houses, and lead captive silly women laden with sins, led away with divers lusts, Ever learning, and never able to come to the knowledge of the truth" (2 Tim. 3:1-7 KJV).

Turnabouts

Though I get very anxious about flying, Judy, Brandon and I have safely returned to American soil after our visit with our oldest son Steven and his family in "Jolly Ole England." I'm glad that my first trip out of the country was to a place that speaks English, even though I did find out that they speak England English but I speak American English which is different, but fun.

Of course there are many things which we saw and learned about, of which I could not tell you all of them today, but will probably have more to say about our trip as the year progresses. But being a car enthusiasts and one who enjoys traveling the observation that I would like to make today is about their roads. I'm sure you already know that they drive on the left side of the road with the steering wheel of the car on the right side and shifter on the left side of the driver. And yes, it is confusing. Not only that, their way of instructing drivers by ways of signs and marking the roads are very different from ours, and on top of all that, you are supposed to know the speed limit without it being posted. Also, the roads are narrow, with hedges, trees and fences right next to the road because they have no shoulders or road right-of-way. So you had better stay awake when driving.

There was one thing about their road system that I did like and think I could get use to. They had almost no "stop signs" and very few "red lights," instead they have "turnabouts." A turnabout could be large or small; there could be two roads intersecting or five. When approaching a turnabout you get into it by going left, while yielding to the traffic that may be already in the turnabout, then you stay in it till you come to the road that you want to travel on, and then you veer to your left once again. I like them because many times when traveling here in the states I pass my turn and have to make a U-turn. But in England you can just continue to go around the turnabout until you decide which turn you would like to make. It makes making a U-turn a lot easier.

The Bible teaches us that the Lord desires to have a relationship with us, yet because He is Holy and we are sinners, we must come through Christ and claim the sacrifice which He paid upon the cruel cross in giving His life. Acts 3:19 says that we are to "Repent therefore and be converted that your sins may be blotted out. . . (NKJV)." Then in Acts 26:29 he says "repent and turn to God, and do works [which gives evidence of] repentance."

When witnessing to a person that they may receive eternal life, we use those verses and explain that repentance is turning to God through Jesus and away from our sin. It's like making a U-turn. Now that I have been through a turnabout, I see that it would even make it easier to explain, because in many places U-turns are illegal and difficult. But when you are confronted with Christ, He offers us a turnabout to which we can turn from our sins and to God through Him. Isn't that so neat, because He makes it so easy? And not only that, we know that we are faced with choices everyday, to which we must make a decision to which way we are turning. With Christ and the Holy Spirit living within us, we don't have to stop at a sign or a light to ponder what we will do next; we can just enter into His Word (the turnabout) that Christ gives us, listen to the leading of the Holy Spirit and continue on in a victorious life through Christ.

You may have just approached a turnabout in your life, please enter into it, for it is "by grace you are saved through faith; and that not of yourselves: it is the gift of God (Ephesians 2:8)" Faith is not just believing facts about Jesus, even the devils believe and tremble (James 2:19). But faith is trusting in Jesus. As I said earlier I am not a good flyer, I get anxious when I know I'm going to be flying. But I have learned through the years, if I'm going to get to some of the places I want to go, the only way to go is to fly, so I have to put my trust in the plan and the pilot. You see, you will never make a trip as I have just done until you trust the plane enough to board it. And you will never receive the peace and joy that the Lord gives as we receive Eternal Life until you turnabout from yourself and sin and turn to Him in faith. Believe me, you will not regret it.

Brownies

This is very unusual for me, sharing something that somebody is sharing that somebody shared with him. But I was telling Judy, my wife, that I didn't have anything on my mind to write about and she shared this with me, that someone had shared with her at work. It's very good, not only because many children and young people are falling into this trap of Satan, but many, many adults are allowing their homes to be destroyed by "little things" "little temptations" as they are. But all Satan wants to do is get a little hold in your life, home, church etc. and he can take it down from there. The following was written by David Kirkwood. May it challenge and encourage you as you face decisions of what you read, watch on TV and Movies and Internet and the music you listen to and the places you go.

David writes, "Some years ago when I was a pastor, I walked into my church office after a Sunday morning service to find a sandwich bag on my desk containing three chocolate brownies. Some thoughtful and anonymous saint who knew my love for chocolate had placed them there, along with a piece of paper that had a short story written on it. I immediately sat down and began eating the first brownie as I read the following story.

"Two teenagers asked their father if they could go to the theater to watch a movie that all their friends had seen. After reading some reviews about the movie on the Internet, he denied their request. 'Aw dad, why not?' They complained. 'It's rated PG-13, and we're both older than thirteen!' Dad replied, 'Because that movie contains nudity and portrays immorality, which is something that God hates, as being normal and acceptable behavior.'

"'But dad, those are just very small parts of the movie! That's what our friends who've seen it have told us. The movie is two hours long and those scenes are just a few minutes of the total film! It's based on a true story and good triumphs over evil, and there are other redeeming themes like courage and self-sacrifice. Even the Christian movie review websites say that!' 'My answer is no, and that is my final answer.' You are welcome to stay home tonight, invite some of your friends over, and watch one of the good videos we have in our home collection. But you will not go and watch that film. End of discussion.'

"The two teenagers walked dejectedly into the family room and slumped down on the couch. As they sulked, they were surprised to hear the sounds of their father preparing something in the kitchen. They soon recognized the wonderful aroma of brownies baking in the oven, and one of the teenagers said to the other, 'Dad must be feeling guilty, and now he's going to try to make it up to us with some fresh brownies. Maybe we can soften him with lots of praise when he brings them out to us and persuade him to let us go to that movie after all.' About that time I began eating the second brownie from the sandwich bag and wondered if there was some connection to the brownies I was eating and the brownies in the story. I kept reading...

"The teens were not disappointed. Soon their father appeared with a plate of warm brownies which he offered to his kids. They each took one. Then their father said, 'Before you eat, I want to tell you something, I love you both so much.' The teen-agers smiled at each other with knowing glances. Dad was softening. 'That is why I've made these brownies with the very best ingredients. I've made them from scratch. Most of the ingredients are even organic: the best organic flour, the best free-range eggs, the best organic sugar, premium vanilla and chocolate.'

"The brownies looked mouth-watering, and the teens began to become a little impatient with their dad's long speech.'But I want to be perfectly honest with you. There is one ingredient I added that is not usually found in brownies. I got that ingredient from our own back yard. But you needn't worry, because I only added the tiniest bit of that ingre-dient to your brownies. The amount of the portion is practically insignificant. So go ahead, take a bite and let me know what you think."

"'Dad, would you mind telling us what that mystery ingredient is before we eat?' 'Why? The portion I added was so small. Just a teaspoonful. You won't even taste it.' 'Come on, dad; just tell us what that ingredient is.' "Don't worry! It is organic, just like the other ingredients.' 'Dad!' 'Well, OK, if you insist. That secret ingredient is organic...dog poop.' I immediately stopped chewing that second brownie and I spit it out into the waste basket by my desk I continued reading, now fearful of the paragraphs that still remained. Both teens instantly dropped their brownies back on the plate and began inspecting their fingers with horror.

"'DAD! Why did you do that? You've tortured us by making us smell those brownies cooking for the last half hour, and now you tell us that you added dog poop! We can't eat these brownies!' 'Why not? The amount of dog poop is very small compared to the rest of the ingredients. It won't hurt you. It's been cooked right along with the other ingredients. You won't even taste it. It has the same consistency as the brownies. Go ahead and eat!' 'No, Dad...NEVER!' 'And that is the same reason I won't allow you to go watch that movie. You won't tolerate a little dog poop in your brownies, so why should you tolerate a little immorality in your movies?'

"We pray that God will not lead us unto temptation, so how can we in good conscience entertain ourselves with something that will imprint a sinful image in our minds that will lead us into temptation long after we first see it? I discarded what remained of the second brownie as well as the entire untouched third brownie. What had been irresistible a minute ago had become detestable. And only because of the very slim chance that what I was eating was slightly polluted. (Surely it wasn't...but I couldn't convince myself.)

"What a good lesson about purity! Why do we tolerate any sin? On the day of the Passover, the Israelites were commanded to remove every bit of leaven from their homes. Sin is like leaven - a little bit leavens the whole lump (1 Cor. 5:6). Jesus, 'our Passover' (1 Cor. 5:7), and sin, don't mix.

An Airman's Prayer

Monday, May 29th, is Memorial Day, a day which is much more than the beginning of summer and a time to burn hot dogs. It's a time to remember the many times that our freedom has been challenged and those who have defended it. It's a day to remember The Boston Tea Party, Gettysburg, Korea, Vietnam, Pearl Harbor, Desert Storm, The USS Cole, 9-11 etc. It's a day, as everyday should be, that we respect and celebrate the freedom that we enjoy because of the grace of God that has been bestowed upon us and the men and women who were and are willing to stand in the gap for the country and the principles that it represents.

To help us all to be mindful of what Memorial Day is all about I would like to share with you a prayer that our oldest son wrote the first time he was in Iraq, and to encourage you to pray for him and others that are there today.

He wrote, "Sometimes I wonder why God made me the way I am. Why am I here away from my family, loved ones and children to fight a war that I don't truly understand? Why do I feel it is necessary to be here when I could be home where love is?

Then I think about what God allowed me to see in town today. I saw the innocent faces of children asking me to help them have rights too. Right then I felt a hurt and a sense of peace come over me. They made me think of our country and all its downfalls. My mind raced. I thought of things like, if this country is based on 'One Nation Under God' then why are there brothers against brothers, why is there racism, and how could a God fearing country kill lives that aren't even born yet? How can a person look up to a country that seems to have lost all its morals? Then I remembered, I have the right to be me. I've made many, many mistakes in my life. Mistakes that have become life lessons that I hope to pass on to my children, but I have the right to make mistakes and learn. Heck, I have the right to learn anything I want to. I have the right to learn, love, to eat and to build on life's experiences. Then is when I found out why God made me an airman. I love this country. I love the freedom to worship the God of creation, and not be scared of the consequences. I love the freedom to be me, to learn from mistakes and not be ridiculed, to be able to live the life God has made for me.

I now have a heart of forgiveness and revenge. I am willing to forgive mistakes. But I am not willing to allow someone to try to take my rights away.

Many people had to die for the rights I enjoy; to those people I am very thankful. They were willing to die for what is right, and that is where I fit into the picture. I am willing to do the same as my forefathers and fight for what is right. I am not willing to back down to someone who wants to rule the world and treat Americans like dogs.

Those children I saw today, wanting freedom showed me who I am, A SPOILED AMERICAN. They long for the day to have freedoms that I take advantage of everyday without a care that someone else had to lay down their life for.

I have come to realize that there is no better country than our own. Why we turn against it, is a question I will probably never have answered, but I will fight to the bitter end for the freedom we share. I promise that to every American.

So, ask me why I fight in this war that just seems to linger on and on, and my answer will be, so that you can ask me that question. Ask me why I would volunteer my life for a country that at times doesn't even know I exist, and I will answer, because I am an airman willing to defend every person in this country, no matter who you are. For I have come to realize that if the enemy is allowed to win then every man, woman, and child will have their rights taken from them. I am not willing to allow that to happen as long as I am alive.

Now to the question I asked at the beginning. Why did God make me the way I am? I've found out. He made me a Defender. I am a defender of the faith as well as a defender of my country, and because of that I am not willing to give up and forget every nation that needs me.

Lord, I pray that as this war carries on that Your hand is on it and all decisions are made by You and in Your time. I pray that Your love can be poured out on all nations and that this country and world will stop pushing You away. I also pray for myself and my brothers and sisters in the service in that You will be with them, and the ones who have fallen in the past few days that You will give strength to their families. I pray that our country, which we are fighting for, stays behind us in everything we do, and that our families and loved ones will know that we love them. Amen."

Wake Up Call!

As life unfolds around us, students of the Bible are finding themselves in exciting times. We have always been able to go to the Old Testament and become excited as we read the prophecies of the Messiah's coming, and then to be able to go to the New Testament and to history (His-story) and see it fulfilled. I have noticed that there is a renewed interest in the book of Daniel and the New Testament prophecies of His imminent return and the seven year tribulation period that is foretold in these scriptures. With the development of events in the Middle East and especially around Baghdad, and the appearing of Babylon in our world, even here in the west, one can hardly hold back the excitement as we see firsthand God unfolding His plan right before our eyes.

To put things in simple terms, the Bible basically teaches that before the end of time as we know it, that there will be a world leader who will come to power and will reign for seven years. The first three and a half years or so he will be able to bring about what will seem to be a time of peace and he will allow the Jews to build their temple and return to bringing their sacrifice to the temple, but after a period of time he will throw the Jews out of the temple and establish an image of himself and force the world to worship it. He will then establish what the Bible refers to as the Mark of the Beast which everyone will have to receive in order buy or sell (live).

With that in mind, I now would like to share with you something that Charles Colson shared in his "Breakpoint" article published in the Florida Baptist Witness on January 26th, and Jack Kinsella in his "Omega Letter" shared on January 19th 2006 on their thoughts and quotes from Iranian president Ahmed Ahmadinejad, who is not only a devout Shiite Muslim, but also known as a Mahdaviat.

Colson defines a Mahdaviat as "one who believes in and prepares the way for the Mahdi. The Mahdi also known as the 'Twelfth Iman,' is the equivalent of messiah: 'restorer of religion and justice who will rule before the end of the world.'"

Kinsella wrote that, "In a November 16th speech in Tehran, to senior clerics who had come from all over the Iran to hear him, the new President said the main mission of his Government was to "pave the path for the glorious reappearance of Iman Mahdi." This you should also know, "The mystical 12th Iman of Shia Islam disappeared as a child in 941AD, and Shia Muslims have awaited his reappearance ever since, believing that when he returns, he will reign on earth for seven years, before bringing about the last Judgment and the end of the world." And there is so much more, but my space is limited. But the thing that stands out to me is that "Ahmadinejad not only believes the 12

Imam's appearance is imminent, he believes that it is his mission to bring about the apocalypse in order to force his early return." And from all reports he is very busy preparing the way.

Did you also know that Buddhists are awaiting the appearance of the 'Lord' Matreya; the Hindus await the 'natural ending of the world' during the 'Kali' Age; In Israel, Jews are preparing for the coming of the Jewish Messiah; there are even secular think-tanks like the "Millennium Institute" which say they take a 'holistic' approach to the coming apocalypse with clients such as General Motors Corp, Action Aid, World Bank, UN Development Program, and The Carter Center, developing country governments and so on; and of course you are aware all the movies and news cast that have been focused on end time events in the last year or so.

As we look at these events and begin to get a clearer understanding that there is an expectation of a coming apocalypse deeply ingrained in the human psychic we should awaken to the opportunities to share the good news of the gospel. But that brings us a sad truth unfolding in the local church which was also foretold in the Revelation of Jesus Christ in chapters 2 and 3. It says that in the last days the church will become a compromising, corrupt, dead, lukewarm church much like the churches at Pergamos, Thyatira, Sardis and Laodicea.

Are we living in the last days? You be the judge. 2nd Timothy 3:1-5 gives a description of what those days will look like, as it says, "This know also, that in the last days perilous times shall come. For men shall be lovers of their own selves, covetous, boasters, proud, blasphemers, disobedient to parents, unthankful, unholy, Without natural affection, truce-breakers, false accusers, incontinent, fierce, despisers of those that are good, Traitors, heady, highminded, lovers of pleasures more than lovers of God; Having a form of godliness, but denying the power thereof: from such turn away (KJV). And then we find the same question asked to Christ as He sat upon the Mount of Olives in Matthew 24:3-5 to which He replied with a great warning ". . . And Jesus answered and said unto them, Take heed that no man deceive you. For many shall come in my name, saying, I am Christ; and shall deceive many."

This is a Wake-Up call, The Lord IS coming, it is imminent. Does this excite you or concern you? If it concerns you, Christ invites you to come to Him and confess your sins and turn from your evil ways (Romans 10:9-13). If it excites, share the Good News with someone today.

Billboard or Light

In our Thirty-three years of marriage the Lord has blessed Judy and I with three sons and seven grandchildren. The boys are now thirty-two, twenty seven and twenty-two. Like all families they all have some family resemblances, as most say they would know they were my sons, even if they were not told, just by meeting them. But they each also have different personalities and likes. The oldest is career Air Force, the middle drills wells, and the youngest works in retail. But if you were to see them when they are not in their work uniforms you would think the middle one was employed by the Georgia Bulldogs and the youngest the Green Bay Packers, because of their clothing. The oldest will be very casual at first glance. You will not see anything on him that will shout, "I'm Air force" but as you get to know him and talk with him you will soon know by his talk and actions that he is all Air Force, and while talking to the other two, you will soon find out who they are.

Personally, I will not pay hard earned money to advertise for anyone as they do. I spent ten years as a radio personality, and was given clothes to wear to promote certain companies, and even at that, they often had to pay me to wear them. I believe first impressions are too important to be hid behind slogans and trademarks, which do not represent the person I really am. Plus I don't feel comfortable wearing T-shirts in public and caps are very uncomfortable to me. I guess that's why God gave me hair.

A couple a weeks ago I mentioned my concern about the clothing the young people will be wearing when they return to school, and shared the interest that I have that all public schools should go to uniforms in order to enhance the education process. Because I feel the message that comes from the person on the inside of the clothing, is more important than the message that comes from the clothing worn by the person.

At this point I will admit to you, that though I don't wear messages and trademarks on my clothing, I do display bumper stickers on my cars. I also admit, they tell you where I stand on certain issues. By pulling up behind my cars you will soon know that I support and pray for our soldiers risking their lives so that I can enjoy these freedoms that I have to speak up on issues that I hold dear. You will also know that I believe that marriage is "One man and One woman for life", no it's or others. You will also know that I love and support the family and children's ministries at our church and that I believe there is Only One Way to Heaven, His name is Jesus Christ. But I also know that because my car may be screaming these great messages, it does not make my car or Me a Christian, but reminds me that my driving should resemble the way that Christ would drive if He were here today.

Actually I have recently been convicted that there are a lot of saved people in America because our forefathers laid a great foundation for us to build on, as they placed "In God We Trust" on our currency to remind us where our strength comes from, and they made Bibles so easy for each of us to obtain, so that we can know "For God so Loved the World that He gave His only begotten Son that Who so ever believes on Him should not perish but have everlasting life" (John 3:16 KJV). And "that if you confess with your mouth the Lord Jesus and believe in your heart that God has raised Him from the dead, you will be saved" (Romans 10:9 NKJV). With people hearing and receiving these messages from God's Holy Word, I believe there may be a lot of people who are saved and when they die they will go to heaven. But on other the hand, I am very, very afraid that in America there aren't any "Christians". Because all around the world "Christian" people who are a living message for Christ and have a family resemblance to Him are being persecuted, imprisoned, tortured and murdered everyday, but not in America. Maybe it is because of the great foundation of freedom of religion that our forefathers lay, which we seem to be slowly losing. Or could it be that we don't have enough family resemblance to Christ that we are worth Satan's trouble. Maybe it is because we are wearing our religion on our shirts and our cars, rather than making an impact with the life we live. You see, in Acts 11:26 the people did not call themselves Christians, but the people who had seen Christ and now knew them, called them Christians, because, they saw Him in them, a great family resemblance.

Billboards that give directions are good, but a life that reflects the Light and leads the way is better (Matthew 5:16). Lord, please give us the strength to not advertise something we are not, but to be known for Whom we belong by the life we live for you everyday.

Extreme Makeover

According to television most people are not happy with themselves. The big thing now coming out of Hollywood is face lifts, tummy tucks and nose jobs. A spin off of this fad, to become someone different than who are, is a program called "Extreme Makeover". They supposedly choose people that seem to not have taken care of themselves or have had some type of misfortune in their life and need work done on their bodies so that they can live a more fulfilled life. So they send them to these doctors who cut here, there and everywhere and they give them a new hair style and new set of clothes. They say it's all about building up these persons' self-esteem. Which I'm sure it may work for a day or two or maybe a year. But these people are put back in the same world they came from, with the same problems they had before. Now there's a program that has spun off that called "Extreme Home Makeover." The few times I watched it I thought it was real neat how they took a family who had experienced some great tragedy, they send this family on a vacation that they could have never afforded, and while they are gone for a week, people come and tear down their house and build one about four times bigger than that one was with all kind of nice extras that a normal family could never afford. Sometimes they leave them with a check for a $100,000 or so for the repair and maintenance that such a house would require, which I thought was very thoughtful. But I still wonder how many real problems of life do these new houses really solve and how many do they actually create?

Since being in the ministry and not really ever owning a home, often times they seem to become a weight to ministers. Because we don't own a home, "Extreme Home Makeover" is not that appealing to me. Now if they had "Extreme, Give A House To Have A Home In", that might work for us. And since I have a perfect body LOL (for those who don't know e-mail talk, LOL means you can laugh out load about the statement just made), I don't need a body make over. Mine may not be perfect or pretty, but I've came sort of fond of it. There is another program along that same line, which I could use; it's called "Overhaul". They come and steal your project vehicle, such as my Jeep Scrambler that I'm working on, and then bring it back completely restored. Now I could get into that for my Jeep or our RV. But actually it would take all the fun out of it being something that I had actually done.

So it seems to me, these programs are real tear jerkers, and we all need a good joyful cry now and then. But are they forgetting something very important that would truly make a real difference in a person's life and in the family? You see, there's an old saying which says "a house does not make a home" and neither does a body make a person. What did the Old Timers used to say? "You can wash a pig and put a ribbon around his neck and bring him in the house, but as soon as he gets a chance he will be right back in the middle of the mud and all muddy again, because that is who he is."

Actually God, Who created man, and established the family, was the originator of the extreme make-over for an individual or a home. It's not a program that one may be on, or attend, or go through; it's not about a religious experience either, but about having a relationship with God through His Son, Jesus Christ. You see, everyone can have a complete, extreme makeover that will not only effect things that can be seen, but also change the inner man from which the problem comes from. It is a change that will not affect you for a month or a year or two, but for all eternity. It will change your outlook about life and about death.

The Bible teaches us that when we agree with God that in ourselves we are helplessly lost and need a Savior (Romans 10:9-13) and allow Him to become the Lord of our lives, all things become new in Him (2 Corinthians 5:17, Therefore if any man be in Christ, he is a new creature: old things are passed away; behold, all things are become new).

Christian Disciple?

While passing a car on I-10, I noticed a bumper sticker that read "I'm a ..." and then it had a name of a political party, which was followed by "and I'm a Christian." I had many thoughts as I read it, such as: "Why do they think they need to defend their actions or who they are?" "Do they think they need to clarify something to someone?" Basically, "Why make such a statement?" Then I was listening to what we nowadays call a "Christian radio station" and they were promoting a "Christian business directory" in which they claimed they listed "Christian Electricians," "Christian Plumber's," "Christian Realtors," etc. If you listen to the news you discover there are people who claim they are "Christian homosexuals," "Christian prostitutes," "Christian alcoholics," and "Christians this" and "Christians that." It seems to me that we have taken a very honorable word "Christian" and began to use it in such way that it has lost it effectiveness and meaning, in that it has actually became a slang word just like the word "Hell." People say "hell" without any thought of the place which does exist as the eternal abode and punishment for those who reject Christ as their Savior. I seriously wonder how many of these "Christians" if put on trial for being a Christian would be convicted? And now we are tacking the word "Christian" on everything so that it no longer means anything.

The Bible says "they were first called "Christians" at Antioch" (Acts 11:26). They were literally making fun of these people because they had a demeanor about them that reminded the person of the demeanor of Jesus Christ as He walked here upon the earth. So let's take something very simple, such as a radio station. Earlier in my life, I made my living for 10 years behind a mike of a radio station and loved it. But the station was made out of wood and bricks and consisted of electronics of which none of these things had a demeanor which made me think of Jesus Christ. Yes, the station was used to share the good news of Christ and most of the employees would tell you that they were "Christians." And that brings me to the next question. Were they "Christian employees" then? Or were they sinners who had been saved by the grace of God? And is it a "Christian radio station" or an instrument by which Disciples of Christ encourage and challenge other Disciples of Christ?

In the Bible, believers and followers of Christ never called themselves "Christians" even though many of them were put to death because of their love for Christ. Yet very few were called "Christians" by people who watched their lives. The Bible also teaches that we should be humble, yet when we use the word "Christian" to set us apart from others, are we showing a demeanor that resembles Christ? I think not.

Personally, I don't think Christ would put a bumper sticker on His car saying He was a Republican, Democrat, Independent or whatever. But I do believe He would vote for the person who would stand for truth and morality regardless of the party, regardless of what others thought. And He would not be ashamed of the stand He took and He would definitely let the ones He voted for, know where He stood and where He expected them to stand. He would vote for people who understand that we are all put here by God for a purpose and that purpose is to do His will, not ours.

Go ahead, I know you want to ask me the question, "Are you a "Christian Preacher?" Well my answer is simple, "What do you think?" I know that I am a sinner saved by the Grace of God (Acts 2:21; Romans 10:9-13) and as I live I have the Holy Ghost living in me and when I die I know I will then be with Christ (Philippians 1:21). I also know that my demeanor is not that which reminds me of Christ always, because at times I don't stand strong and firm on things as I should, and at other times I am not as humble, loving and caring as I think He was. But it is my desire to be more like Him each and every day, so that makes me a disciple of Christ, my Lord and Savior (1 Peter 4:16). I know that many of these people who I mentioned at the first may be saved, because they have repented of their sins at one time and confessed Christ as their Lord. But to call themselves a "Christian" is say they are obedient to the Word of God as Christ was even to His death on the Cross. And many of those mentioned are not obedient even to deny themselves of things of this world, or they wouldn't have to put the suffix "Christian" in front of their title to tell others who they are. For when we are obedient to God and His word, and have the demeanor of Christ, others will add it for us.

So Much Static

Recently I carried a couple who had been stranded in Bonifay down to Cape Canaveral. It's about a seven hour trip one way, and I was determined to go and get back in one day. So on the way back I did something that I'm sure is very unusual, because I had never done it before. I tried tuning in a radio station way before I was close enough to receive a signal from it. I'm sure you have come to the conclusion that I was traveling alone, because if anyone had been with me, it would have drove them crazy. I say that because normally when I am traveling, I'll tune in a station that I like and leave it there until it is so fuzzy you can't understand what anyone is saying, and it drives my family nuts. Since I have traveled quite a bit throughout Florida, Georgia and Alabama I have favorite stations already picked out that I will pick up as one fades out. But sometimes there are areas where I drive through that there is not a station I like, so I just listen to static until I get close to the next one. Well, there is one of those places between the I-75 and I-10 interchange and Tallahassee. But this time instead of listening to static of the station I was listening to, I decided to tune in the station that I was approaching and listen to their static. To my surprise the station was not on the air, but I knew the next station in Marianna was on the same frequency, so I just left it there. Listening to static as long as

I did that evening would have actually driven my family bonkers, probably you also. But it actually made my trip interesting and gave me something to write about.

As I was trying to listen to a station that was out of reach, other stations on the same frequency that were further away and probably more powerful would bleed in from time to time, I picked up a station out of Texas for a while and then one out of North Carolina. But during that time I began to think of my relationship with Christ, my Lord and Savior, and the spiritual condition of this great nation we live in. Most people think that when they desire to pray, all they have to do is pray and God will hear and answer their prayers. But actually that is not what the Bible teaches about prayer. It teaches us that before God hears our prayers, we must come through His Son, Jesus Christ and His righteousness, and as we approach Him we must be repentant and our request must be within His will (James 1:5-8,17; 4:2-3; 5:13-18; John16:23-24; Psalms 66:18; Hebrews 3:16-19; 1 Peter 3:7-12).

So basically these scripture teach us that when we are not following the Lord and being obedient to His direction for our life, He does not hear us. And it goes on to say in the Bible that our ears become dull to hearing Him (too much static and interference from other things). When churches and church organizations are defrocking priest, bishops and pastors because they speak out against sins such as homosexuality, adultery, fornication, abortion, etc. and people are getting divorces and destroying the family while saying God approves of it, we have people, churches and a nation who are not tuned into the right leadership, for they are basically writing their own Bibles. The Bible as it stands is God's Holy Word and the only authority by which we must stand and teach others. Instead of letting the static of His direction and His will fade in the background, we need to turn around (repent) and began to travel toward Him.

At one time in my life I begin to try to get a pilots license. So I began to study the wind flow charts and learn about plotting my course. I remember someone pointing out the radio in the cockpits of the small planes and a list of AM radio stations to which you could plot your flights by their signal. It went something like I have previously mentioned, as you planned your trip, you would find a station nearby and fly toward the signal. Do you have your life-flight pattern focused on the right and true signal which will not only give you eternal life through Christ after this life, but will also help you stay on a peaceful, joyful pattern through all the storms of life? If not, dust off the Bible, read it and apply to your life.

Pagan Church

If you understand the meaning of these two words, "pagan" and "church", then you know they do not, or should not, be words that appear together, because they are opposites. Even though a lot of buildings have signs on them proclaiming they are a church, it is not the proper use of the word, even though it can be the place where the "church" assembles. For, in my humble opinion, the word "church" represents individuals who have become slave servants to the Lord Jesus Christ thus living according to His Word, and allowing Him to direct their lives (Romans 1:1, Jude 1, John 14:15; 23-24). But on the other hand, the word "pagan" represents that which is opposed to the Lordship of Christ and His Word, the Bible.

Yet in the book of The Revelation, God describes for us what can be interpreted as a pagan church. As one begins to study the book of The Revelation of Jesus Christ, we soon discover that it was written for the purpose of revealing Christ. The first chapter tells of the things that Christ has done, as He came to the earth. Chapters two and three tells of things that are now taking place, in what is called the age of grace or the church age. Chapters four through the remainder of the book tell us of things that are yet to take place, things that will take place after the church has been removed.

The churches that are named in chapters two and three are actual churches that existed in the time of Paul, in what we now call Turkey. The problems that Paul makes reference to in each church actually existed. But as you study history, you can see how that these churches represent the church as it has played its part in history, and you can see the influence that each of these have had on the church as we know it today. And since the Bible tells us that each believer is the Temple of the Lord (2 Corinthians 6:14-16, Ephesians 2:21), we can also examine ourselves to see which of these seven churches you and I are as an individual, to hear the warning and blessings from the Lord that the Lord had for us.

With the holidays soon approaching, especially Halloween and Santa Claus, it seems that we should look at the church that many have called the pagan church, the church in Thyatira, found in Revelation 2:18-29. This church had followed the church of Smyrna of Revelation 2:8-11, which was the persecuted church of AD 100-313. Satan thought he would destroy the church through great persecution, but the church grew stronger, in spite of the persecution. So Satan decided he would join the church, which he did at the church of Pergamos of Revelation 2:12-17, a time in history around AD 313, when Constantine began to patronize the church. In 378 AD, Theodocius, the Roman Emperor went as far as to declare that everybody was now a Christian. Even today you can ask people if they are a Christian, and they will answer, "for sure, I'm an American aren't' I?" Of course I know that those reading this know you are not a Christian because you are born in America, or into a Christian home. Salvation is a personal relationship between you and the Lord Jesus Christ, after one has repented their sins and received Him as their Lord and Master (Acts 3:19; 26:20, Romans 10:9-10).

That brings us to the church at Thyatira, the pagan church of the dark years of AD 590 through 1517, a time in history when the state had begun to pay the bills of the church. So in order to please the state, they brought certain pagan practices from the pagan Roman temples right into the churches and all kinds of off-the-wall doctrines entered the church. They even began to deny the finished work of Jesus Christ on the cross of Calvary. The church became filled with paganism and with sin and shame. It had very little resemblance to what the Bible teaches. Actually the church became to look more like the world than a people dedicated to serving Christ. And because the church no longer resembled that which Christ had died for, many of the cults of our day were formed as a revolt against pagan Christianity.

One of the places to see paganism in the church is to look at what you celebrate.

Yes some holiday's observances we have may be good, especially as people become grateful for the many blessings we do enjoy here in America, and the opportunity that Christians have to remind the world that God sent His Son to this world to redeem it. As the holidays approach, may this be a time that the world will see a Christ like church, not a pagan church.

The End of Time

As a boy attending a mission in downtown Chicago, I remember the times that the preacher would preach on the Rapture of the Church, the Tribulation Period and the End of Time. I remember being concerned about these things because I was just getting familiar with this world that I was in. Because I was a child at that time, many things didn't make sense to me. Many people ask me now, "Didn't that big city scare you then?" To which I have to answer, no, because that was all that I knew, and as far as I was concerned, I owned the city, and it was a great place because it was home. Not many things bothered me back then, but I would get concerned when I thought about the "end of time" because I was so familiar with things as they were and it was hard to conceive of things being any different.

Several years ago, while a pastor in north Georgia, I was invited to take the "Emmaus Walk". The Emmaus Walk is sponsored by Methodist churches around the world and it is what I call one of the most wonderful spiritual renewing week-ends that anyone can take. Actually I have been able to go three times, because I was invited back to minister on two other occasions. There are many things that are very special about the walk; some of them I won't share because it would spoil the walk for you, if you are ever invited. But I will mention one thing about it that taught me a great lesson on the "end of time". While on your walk you have no access to watches, clocks, calendars, phones or anything that will remind you of time, or things taking place outside your walk. It is the most blessed time once you get over the withdrawal pains, to have no concept of time, other than that of nature and what your body tells you.

Now as a middle-aged person, as our society calls us, time has become such a big factor in my life. As I'm writing, I am writing because there is a dead-line in which I must have this submitted by. And just as every week, the next time I turn around it will be Sunday again, and then again, and then again because that is when I must have something from the Lord (hopefully) to feed the congregation that calls me their pastor. Your day, as mine, may be Monday or Friday, a day in which certain things must be done whether you are ready or not. It is just remarkable how short seven days in a week and twenty-four hours in a day have become. According to the calendar it is already March 2006; what happened to 2004? I must have gone to sleep, but I know I didn't.

Now when I think of eternity, I get excited. Because "eternity" is what will take place when time is no more (the end of time). As you read the Revelation of Jesus Christ from God's Holy Word and you come to chapter 21, you come to a time in which the Lord has promised will come, the end of time, when there will be no more time pieces of any kind, because we will be in an eternal state, in new eternal bodies (Praise the Lord) if you received Christ into your life.

The "time" that we now experience, has been given to us as a gift from God, in which He allows us to choose which eternal state we desire to spend eternity in. Because to my understanding, there are two; one which I refer to as eternal death, where all who have rejected Christ as their Lord will be resurrected in the same body in which they died, with all the cravings and pains they had in this life, to die eternally but never dying. On the other hand if a person has given their life to Christ and allowed Him to be the master and Lord of their life, they will receive a new body, likened to the body that Christ had after His resurrection, one in which we will live and reign with Him throughout eternity.

Can you now see why I get excited when I think about eternity? Have you opened your Bible lately as you watch the news? It seems as if the end of time is not far away. No more time, what a thought! Read it for yourself; it's exciting. Read Revelation 20 and 21, Romans 5:12, 6:23, 10:9-13, John 3:16-20; you won't regret it.

Ticking Clock

Did you see on the news, or read about the "Doomsday Clock" in Chicago? Most of the networks seemed to carry the story, though they didn't seem to spend much time on the story, just a brief mention.

First of all, I had heard of it, but really didn't think it existed; but apparently it does. It seems that scientists created the clock in 1947 to access the threat of a nuclear holocaust during the Cold War and it was placed at the University of Chicago.

The story that made the news is that on Wednesday, January 17, 2007 scientists changed the time on the clock during a dual ceremony in London and Washington. The clocks minute hand was moved forward two minutes closer to midnight, which symbolizes the apocalypse. The time on the "Doomsday Clock" now reads five minutes to midnight. According to Heather Scroops of Fox News, the "Scientists based their decision on countries increasingly seeking nuclear technology, the United States' and Russia's ability to readily launch 2,000 of their 25,000 nuclear weapons, as well as threats posed by global warming, bioterrorism and an overall increase in worldwide terrorism, .."

As I have mentioned in earlier articles, we are living in an interesting and exciting time in history (His-story). As scientists from this report have basically joined "the three Monotheistic Religions of the world who are all anticipating a great event to take place very soon" as I shared with you 1-10-07 that, "Not only are conservative Christians eagerly looking for the return of Christ to take His Bride, the Church, out, which will then usher in the seven year reign of the anti-christ, the Jews are also eagerly awaiting the return of the Messiah to establish His kingdom. And the reason we are seeing so much in the news about Muslims since 9-11, is that Muslims are awaiting the return of the 'Twelfth Iman,' believing that when he returns, he will reign on earth for seven years, before bringing about the last Judgment and the end of the world."

Hopefully somebody is reading this and asking "Well, what can we do or what should we be doing?" To which I would have to answer, "The answer is simple." If you're a disciple of Jesus Christ, look up for your redemption is very near at hand. But don't just go around with your head up in the air looking for His return, but be busy sharing His love with everyone who will listen, so they too will be ready to go up before the end comes, and meet Christ in the air. If you're not a disciple of Christ and you have not received His truth, I'd either get me a good hold on this world and its view of things, because it's soon going to become a bumpy ride. Or I would find me a Bible, begin to read and accept the Truth in it, (the book of John is a good place to start) then find someone who is living a life that resembles the life of Christ that you find in the Bible, and ask them to introduce you to Him. And I'm sure you will find that, that person is active in a church near-by, and you should join them as they worship our Lord, Who was crucified for our sins, rose victoriously winning the victory over sin, death and hell and is soon returning for His bride, His Church.

Yes, to some it's a time to be concerned, while to others it's an exciting time. As you read your Bible, you will also find that Christ said the first time He was here on earth that ".. there shall be signs in the sun, and in the moon, and in the stars; and upon the earth distress of nations, with perplexity; the sea and the waves roaring; Men's hearts failing them for fear, and for looking after those things which are coming on the earth: for the powers of heaven shall be shaken. And then shall they see the Son of man coming in a cloud with power and great glory. And when these things begin to come to pass, then look up, and lift up your heads; for your redemption draweth nigh" (Luke 21:25-28 KJV). You may also wonder how it will take place. That is also recorded for us in the scriptures, as it says "For the Lord Himself shall descend from heaven with a shout, with the voice of the archangel, and with the trump of God: and the dead in Christ shall rise first: Then we which are alive and remain shall be caught up together with them in the clouds, to meet the Lord in the air: and so shall we ever be with the Lord." "Wherefore comfort one another with these words"

(1st Thessalonians 4:16-18 KJV). But actually for the time that it will all take place, the Bible tells us that no one knows the time but the Father in Heaven (Mark 13:32-37). But if you're one of His disciples, this you know, it's a great trip! So live like you know Him, if you do, and enjoy the trip while sharing His love with others. Because it won't be a doomsday but a celebration day!

Through the Eyes

Last week Jason, my little brother, (I guess I can call him that since he is twenty years younger than I am), sent me an E-mail. In this E-mail he was sharing with me an article that he had written for their church newsletter. I'd like to share his article with you all, because it's good.

Jason writes, "A while back as Kelsey my daughter and I were coming back from somewhere by ourselves in the car, something happened I almost missed. Kelsey is sort of a daydreamer. She can stare out a window for hours and never say a word. Well this was one of those times. It was a beautiful day with large white clouds in the sky. As we drove quietly listening to the radio, she turned from the window and proceeded to ask this question. 'Dad, is Jesus coming back today?' Startled, I looked up to see what she saw and said, 'I don't know Kelsey, and no one knows when Jesus is coming back.' Her response was unique to say the least. She said, 'I hope He does, I like Jesus.'"

Jason goes on to share, "I remember the happenings of that day vaguely but I probably only looked up in the sky once if any. The trouble of life had my mind tuned out to my surroundings, and I was blinded to the possibility of Christ' return. But if no one else that day was watching for Him, Kelsey was. Not out of fear or dread was she searching the sky, but out of joy. She wasn't longing for one more day on earth to finish up a last minute report; she was just eager to meet someone she had heard a lot about. I truly believe something inside of her knows as truth, what so many hopes is only a myth."

"Ever since that day I have found myself looking up more often, wondering if Jesus is coming today. Wanting to see Him, not fearing the end, but longing for a new beginning."

Jason concludes this thought with two scripture references. Please read them, then look and ask yourself are you truly anxious about the return of Christ? If the answer is no then you need to consider why not? For today is the day of Salvation, we are not promised tomorrow.

"But of that day and hour no one knows, not even the angels of heaven, but My Father only. Matthew 24:36.

"Watch therefore, for you know neither the day nor the hour in which the Son of Man is coming. Matthew 25:13

Join with me today in looking up and anticipation of His return for His Bride, the Blood bought, born again Church.

The End of the Beginning

Through the years as I meet people who have read these articles but never attended the church that I pastor, they will sometimes ask, "If I came to hear you preach, would I hear the same thing that I read in the paper?" They then looked surprised when I say "no". Through the years I have always tried to keep my preaching, teaching and writing to have their each individual purpose. Probably the main reason I keep them separate is that it is hard to write while moving around and fluctuating my voice as I do when I preach or teach. But I am sure there are times when one may influence the other, such as this week. For the past ten months the Lord has led me to preach fifty messages from the book of Acts, and that was only after thirty-three messages from the book of John.

While preaching through the book of John, we were able to witness the awesome life of Christ our Lord, and hear Him preach and teach as only He can. In the book of Acts we were able to witness the birth of His Church and witness its struggles and victories. And as everyone knows who has ever read their Bible, in Acts we are able to witness the conversion of Saul, the hater of Christianity, to Paul, the obedient servant of Christ as he and the early church literally turned the world up side down while being persecuted and even slain for the sake of the Gospel they preached and lived.

Through the years I have lost count of how many times that I have read the Bible through, but every time I come to Acts 28:31, I began to search for the rest of the book. Because, basically it seems to me that Dr. Luke, the writer of the book of Acts, leaves us hanging off of a cliff wanting more. When we get to this point we have traveled with Paul all around the world. We have stood with him as he has stood before Felix, Festus and Agrippa, who had basically held him as a political prisoner for over two years. He appeals to stand before Caesar and we travel with him through his third shipwreck and endless storms. As we come to chapter 28 of Acts he has spent months upon the rough seas and stranded on an island, and has traveled hundreds of miles on land, only again to sit two more years as a political prisoner waiting to stand before Caesar. The book ends as a large crowd is leaving his room, arguing about the message of the gospel and truth which he has shared. Dr. Luke fails to tell us what happened to the church at Rome that Paul was so eager to get to, so he could encourage them, and he fails to tell us of Paul's fate.

As a child in Chicago, Illinois, I will always remember not only having "Fire Drills", but also "Air Raid Drills", where we would all hunker down in the school's hallways with our head between our legs up against the wall. As a child it frightened me at the thought of such a raid. But as I read history I begin to understand the purpose. Part of the reason for such a drill went back to November of 1942 in London, as Hitler's forces had invaded the skies and darkness covered them heavier than ever before. The frequent air raids and blackouts had everyone's nerves frayed as they continually would scrabble for shelter as the bombs would come, and then more bombs and more bombs and more bombs. As the British clung to each other through the night, what could their Prime Minister, Winston Churchill say that could steel the people's melting courage? Well, on November 10th, at a Mayor's day luncheon, he slowly spoke these immortal words. "Now this is not the end. It is not even the beginning of the end. But it is, perhaps, the end of the Beginning." And of course, the rest is history, as they say.

Perhaps there is a Divine reason that God did not allow Dr. Luke to finish writing the book of Acts in his day. Maybe, just maybe, could it be that it is yet to be completed, because it is basically the story of His Church. Maybe the book of Acts is just the "End of the Beginning."

Satan tried to destroy the church bought by the blood of Christ in its infancy, by taking the followers of Christ such as Paul, be-heading some, boiling some, feeding some to the lions in the arenas, even keeping some as political prisoners. But His followers were strengthened and encouraged by His life and immortal words "I will build My church, and the gates of Hell shall not prevail against it" (Matthew 16:18 NKJV). Today I believe it is safe to say that the book of Acts (*His story* of His Church) is still being written in the portals of heaven, and books around the world, as He continues to build, encourage and strengthen all who look to Him and believe. "For God so loved the World that He gave His only begotten Son, that who ever believes in Him will not perish, but have everlasting life" (John 3:16 paraphrased).

The Plan

As I was making my way through the church Sunday morning, greeting and shaking hands with all who had came to worship, and having some small talk, I came to Coach Kindig and his family, and as usual he gave me his firm appreciated handshake. As he shook my hand and greeted me by looking at me while we shook hands he said, "The man with the plan." As that familiar greeting reached the thinking part of my brain, (yes, there is a small part there, somewhere) I thought and told him, "I like that, but with the emphasis on The Plan." The man with <u>The Plan</u>"; think about it. That would be a good thing to be said about all Christians.

There are a lot of people with plans. Families have vacation plans and reunion plans. Builders and people who desire to build something have a plan. Many people have a plan of how they are going to get to where they desire to get to in life. I understand that the Taliban, because of their religious beliefs have a plan to rid the world of the heathens, as they call America, because they consider us a Christian nation. President Bush and our soldiers around the world have a plan to protect freedom and offer it to as many people and nations as possible. Young couples dream and make plans for the future, and many older people have that plan to retire.

Not all plans are good plans, and not many plans are actually able to be seen through and finished as they originally began. But there is one plan that God intended to be shared with every person in the world, for simplicity we will call it, The Plan of Salvation, which I guess we could say, is The Plan of Plans. And in reality it is a very simple plan that even children can understand. Yet, so many stumble all over it, because it is so simple; it truly defines love and acceptance.

Jesus Christ, the only Son of God, came and placed the plan in motion, and is in retrospect The Plan. Christ said He did not come to destroy, but to fulfill. The plan is built around God's love for all people, and His desire to have a wonderful relationship with them. As He says in John 3:16, "For God so loved the world, that he gave his only begotten Son, that whosoever believeth in him should not perish, but have everlasting life" (KJV). Here's The Plan. As you have seen, and should understand, God loves you, and desires that you have a wonderful, eternal relationship with Him. That is why Christ said John 14:3, . . "if I go and prepare a place for you, I will come again, and receive you unto myself; that where I am, there ye may be also." But in reality, on our own we cannot come to God, because He is Holy and we are sinners, Romans3:10-23. That is why we sing and talk about His amazing love and grace. You see He tells us in Romans 5:8, even when we were sinners, which are basically an enemy of God, that He (Christ) gave us His love in that He died that we might have life and have it even more abundantly. You see, the penalty for our sin is death, but through Christ, He offers us Eternal Life (Romans 6:23). The only way to receive eternal life is by grace through faith, because it is the gift of God (Ephesians 2:8). You can receive your gift from God by simply confessing with your mouth the Lord Jesus, and believing in your heart that God has raised Christ from the dead, and He says you shall be saved. Because "it is with the heart man believeth unto righteousness; and with the mouth confession is made unto salvation." Romans 10:9-10.

That is why I like "The man with The Plan" and I hope that you have received The Plan, and will share it with someone today. There is no other plan. Jesus Christ, said in John 14:6, "I am the way, the truth, and the life: no man cometh unto the Father, but by me." And I believe once you receive and understand The Plan and what it truly means to you and what it could mean to others if they only had The Plan, you will want to share it with everyone, and you will desire to meet with others who have The Plan that we might worship Him together.

Insurance

One of the most aggravating parts about being self-employed is the responsibility of finding and purchasing your own health insurance. Of course the truth of the matter is, the purchase of auto, home, life.... any type of insurance is a hard thing to do. I think you understand what I'm trying to say is, that big hunk of money that either comes out of a paycheck or you have to pay personally to the insurance companies and taxes, seems like money that is being thrown away.

The thing that makes it so difficult is the understanding of actually what is taking place. You see the insurance company is gambling that you will not need them to pay off for what they have you insured for, and you are gambling that you will need them to protect you from losing your shirt should a catastrophe take place in your life. But to protect their interest the insurance company charges you a very high premium so that you can feel good that you have protection, while at the same time they protect themselves by excluding anything that they see that might cause them to have to pay out. On top of that, they have the nerve to make you pay a deductible first and then when they do pay out, they only pay a percentage of what your need will be.

The truth is, they know they have you, because without insurance you're taking such a great risk.

Basically you're living very dangerously to not carry insurance, but to carry insurance adds a great hardship to your life, which actually puts you between a rock and a hard place. When I pay those insurance premiums I think of the difficulties that occur because I pay them, while on the other hand, the severe consequences of not paying them.

Recently, while being aggravated with the agony of purchasing insurance my mind wondered to something similar but very different, Assurance. I became thankful because of the joy that I have the Assurance that everyone can have in Christ. Assurance comes from accepting the great gift of salvation, which has been made available by God the Father through the blood of His Son, Jesus Christ to all who will receive it.

Assurance, unlike insurance, is easy to obtain; the great price has already been paid. Personally I don't understand why anyone would want to live, and especially why anyone would think of dieing, without the Assurance of Eternal Life that has been bought by the righteousness of Christ. For to die trusting in your goodness, or righteousness, means to meet with the consequences of great agony for all Eternity.

Insurance can both be an agony to have and not to have. Assurance of Eternal life through Jesus Christ is a joy to receive, a joy to share, brings joy to have and will be a wonderful joy and blessings for all eternity. Those who will not receive this wonderful gift are the ones who live in agony. Do you have Assurance and a personal relationship with Christ? You can, and it begins with a simple prayer from your heart. A simple salvation prayer from the heart can be something like this; "Dear Jesus, I believe that You died on the cross for my sins and that You arose from the grave. I now ask You to forgive me of my sins and save my soul. Amen."

Once you've prayed such a prayer and felt His saving power, share it with someone you know, who knows Christ that they might help you grow in your new relationship with Him. Please don't be ashamed of this great event that has taken place in your life, then share this wonderful event with someone you know who may not have this Assurance, they will thank you for all Eternity. (1 John 5:13; John 3:16; Romans 3:10,23; 5:12, 5:8; 6:23; 10:9-13)

PERSONAL TESTAMONY OF AUTHOR

Timothy James Hall, Pastor Gully Springs Baptist Church, Bonifay Florida since February of 2006. Born January 11, 1956 in a small town known as Trion, which is a Cotton Mill town in north Georgia. At my birth, my dad was 20 and my mother 16. They tried to make it in this small town, but felt God leading them to move to Chicago, Illinois soon after my birth. In Chicago we lived on the north side just off Lake Shore Drive. Dad had several jobs, finally settling with Harper Steel.

We began to attend a little Baptist Mission, The Bible Baptist Church, which to get to; you had go into a back alley and then go upstairs over a Pool Hall and Bar. The church met in what once was a Dance Hall. While attending Bible Baptist, the Lord called my Dad to be a preacher. The church ordained him, as he and the pastor felt led to begin another mission on Clark Street, just a few blocks from the Cub's Stadium. This mission, Calvary Baptist Church, did have a ground floor entrance. It was placed in the storefront of an apartment building. They worked hard to clean up the building, and were able to get pews, two pianos, a pipe organ, doors, paneling and an altar from a Catholic church, which was being torn down to build a new building on the other side of Chicago. At that Catholic altar in a place that once was a burned out bar is where I met the Lord on a Sunday morning at the age of twelve.

When I was in the sixth grade, during the Christmas break, we moved back to Trion, because of my Dad's health. There I found things to be tougher than I thought, because now in the South, I was a Yankee in a small town in Georgia, at the age when children are very cruel. A couple of years later, Dad began to pastor again as he worked in the cotton mill. He became the pastor of a congregation of about thirty-five people who called themselves the Wayside Baptist Church.

There at the age of fifteen they allowed me the opportunity to begin growing in the Lord. I began to teach a Sunday school class of people older than myself, and lead the Adult Choir and sing in a trio.

There in the pastorium I would spend many nights listening to a man, which went by the name of Happy Howard on WDOD-FM out of Chattanooga, Tennessee, play Southern Gospel music. You could tell he really enjoyed what he was doing.

One evening my Dad came in from a meeting that he had been to, at an elementary school where Governor Lester Maddox, the governor at that time of Georgia, had spoke. I heard my Dad repeat part of his speech that he gave to those children at that school that stuck with me. He said, "Set your goals so high you know you can't reach them. Then, work toward those goals, giving God the glory for all that was accomplished." At the age of fifteen I aspired to become a DJ on WDOD, playing gospel music and witnessing. I then began to work toward that goal, learning all I could by reading and going to our local radio station and bugging them to death with questions. Before I turned sixteen I had passed the FCC Licensing Test, (which was a lot more difficult then, than it is today). I went to WDOD, which laughed and told me that I had to have experience before they would hire me. I could not understand how I would get experience if they didn't hire me. This really confused me. I continued high school and working at the Piggly Wiggly until I got a job at WRIPAM-FM-TV. That was an accomplishment for a boy of seventeen. Just after I finished high school WDOD did call, offered me a job, which I accepted. While working at WDOD, if you can call it work, (because, man, I was happy), I could witness for Christ, get paid for it, talk to thousands of people and they couldn't talk back. At that same time the Lord also used me as a Sunday school teacher and Youth Choir Director at the Ridge Crest Baptist Church in Rossville, Georgia, where I married the girl of my dreams, Judy. The Lord was so good to me.

A year after we got married, Judy was expecting our first son. WDOD decided there was more money in rock-and-roll than in Gospel. Needless to say, I left, went back to Trion and to work at the Piggly Wiggly. I dabbled in this and that trying to reestablish myself and trying to get my own radio station. During that time the Lord used us, at the Mt. View Baptist Church in Trion, Georgia as Sunday school teachers, Adult and Youth Choir Director for three Years. The Lord then called us to serve at the Ridgeway Baptist Church in Lafayette, Georgia, as Youth Director, and Children's Church Director. While at Ridgeway I got into my own publishing company, which I lost my shirt in. It was at Ridgeway, during the Watch Night Service of 1980, while singing a solo that I surrendered to follow the Lord as He had called me to preach. I had fought this calling for over four years, but there that night, I confessed to the Lord that I was not a preacher and could never preach but would allow Him to preach through me. I confessed it that night, not only to the Lord but also to that congregation. The Lord then began to open doors.

After several years of preaching throughout North Georgia, the Fellowship Baptist Church in Trion asked me to fill their pulpit, and then later called me to be their pastor. I had asked the Lord not to allow them to call me, but He did. You see, the Fellowship Baptist Church, though an older church only had four active members. With my wife and boys we doubled the congregation when we joined them. A church that should have closed its doors years ago according to the world began to grow and so did I. Our one deacon, three members, my wife and the Lord helped work the ministry of this church as I worked two jobs, sometimes three and try to be a pastor. The Lord blessed and in a little over a year we had as many as forty for church and five active Sunday School Classes. Again God was so good. It was while at Fellowship that I met Dr Larry Draper, who was at that time pastor of the West Rome Baptist church in Rome, Georgia. He became a mentor as he led West Rome to pay for much of my seminary work at Luther Rice Seminary in Lithonia, Georgia.

Quickly, to bring you up to date, Judy and I now have three boys, and seven grandchildren (2008). I have been the Pastor of four churches in Georgia. All which were churches that ran less than a hundred in Sunday school and were located in rural areas, but churches that God had ordained to minister to their communities, and which God tremendously blessed as we strived to lead them to be Great Commission Churches. In 1998 the Lord brought us to Florida and the Blue Lake Baptist Church in Chipley where we served as senior pastor for 9 years. In February 2007 the Lord led us to accept an invitation from the Gully Springs Baptist Church to become their senior pastor. God is truly blessing as we strive also to be a Great Commission Church.

I feel the reason the Lord has burdened me so deeply with this book, is because the average church has become unfocused. We have come to the conclusion that "big" is where God is working. We have forgotten that ninety percent of God's churches across America have less than one-hundred people in worship in their average Sunday morning services and that most of their pastors also work to support themselves. What we don't realize is that these men and these churches have the greatest advantage of reaching their community for Christ than anyone else. My burden is for the congregations around the world, and their pastors, that as they get a glimpse of Hell, they will see the lostness of their friends, they then will begin to turn the world up-side for Christ.

Printed in the United States
213203BV00001B/2/P

9 781607 912194